PURE KNITS

PURE KNITS

Sophisticated Designs in Shades of White

YAHAIRA FERREIRA

LARK BOOKS
A Division of Sterling Publishing Co., Inc.
New York / London

Editors: Brian Sawyer and Kathleen McCafferty

Managing Editors: Rebecca Springer and Aimee Chase

Technical Editors: Elaine Gross and K.J. Hay

Photographer: Allan Penn

Stylist: Jennifer Dunlea

Art Director: Wendy Simard

Interior Designer: 3&Co.

Cover Designer: Chris Bryant

Library of Congress Cataloging-in-Publication Data

Ferreira, Yahaira.
Pure knits : sophisticated designs in shades of white / Yahaira Ferreira.
-- 1st ed.
p. cm.
Includes index.
ISBN-13: 978-1-60059-302-4 (pb-with flaps : alk. paper)
1. Knitting--Patterns. I. Title.
TT820.F466 2008
746.43'2041--dc22
2008001512

10 9 8 7 6 5 4 3 2 1

First Edition

Published by Lark Books, A Division of
Sterling Publishing Co., Inc.
387 Park Avenue South, New York, NY 10016

Distributed in Canada by Sterling Publishing,
c/o Canadian Manda Group, 165 Dufferin Street
Toronto, Ontario, Canada M6K 3H6

Distributed in the United Kingdom by GMC Distribution Services,
Castle Place, 166 High Street, Lewes, East Sussex, England BN7 1XU

Distributed in Australia by Capricorn Link (Australia) Pty Ltd.,
P.O. Box 704, Windsor, NSW 2756 Australia

If you have questions or comments about this book,
please contact:
Lark Books
67 Broadway
Asheville, NC 28801
828-253-0467

Manufactured in China

ISBN 13: 978-1-60059-302-4

For information about custom editions, special sales, premium and corporate purchases, please contact Sterling Special Sales Department at 800-805-5489 or specialsales@sterlingpublishing.com.

Contents

Introduction

Every season, a new crop of rich and radiant fashion-inspired colors appear from yarn companies to entice us. Color can bring both joy and fear to some knitters' hearts. The possibility of choosing or combining the "wrong" color from the sometimes overwhelming wall of yarn can be stifling. How liberating would it be to dive into *sumptuous* designs entirely in a winter–white palette?

Think of *Pure Knits* as a palate cleanser of sorts, the sherbet between courses, which lets the knitter's imagination run wild. Once we remove color, we can focus on the hand of the fiber, the texture of the fabric, and the structure of the fit: everything that makes a classic piece heirloom worthy.

White is luxurious in its purity and simplicity, symbolic of special occasions, elegance, and optimism. White brings to mind the extraordinary as well as the ordinary. Not only does it say crisp and clean, but it is also warm and comforting. In one incarnation, it can connote innocence, while in another it can knock 'em dead. No other color can evoke so many different emotions for so many people.

It's funny to think that while I work on a "pure white" book, I'm also planning my wedding. My days are spent thinking about whether I should go with diamond white or ivory, and what colors will best stand out against that particular white. No, this isn't a "wedding knits" book, but some of the same ideas could apply to everyday knitting. You can tie together your look with the other colors you wear; wearing white will make the other colors that much more dramatic.

The patterns in this book bring forth classic lines with a modern edge. The book is broken into chapters based on the techniques used. The chapter Pure White shows you how to add twists to your knitting to create projects that are anything but simple. Cool Textures brings knits and purls to the forefront. Whether highlighting a neckline or used in an allover pattern, Wintry Lace has you covered. From a baby set to a man's Aran, Arctic Cables satisfies your addiction to twists and turns—with or without a cable needle.

Wear white with sophistication. There are plenty of shades to choose from.

CHAPTER 1

Pure White

RETRO PICOT

VÉRONIQUE HAEGELI

A plush cardigan blends vintage flair with a modern fit in a luxurious alpaca yarn. This cardigan is knit in one piece without any seams. The lower piece is knit in one piece from the bottom edge up, with the edge stitches placed on a holder until they are grafted to the upper body and sleeves. The sleeves are worked in the round, and the slant of the V-neck is achieved with short rows.

SKILL LEVEL

Experienced

SIZES

XS (S, M, L, XL)
30 (34, 38, 42, 46)"/
76 (86, 97, 107, 117) cm
Shown in size S

FINISHED MEASUREMENTS

Underbust: 30 (32, 34, 36, 38)"/
76 (81, 86, 91, 97) cm
Bust (with 1–3" of ease):
31 (35, 39, 43, 47)"/
79 (89, 99, 109, 119) cm

MATERIALS AND TOOLS

Yarn

870 (870, 1015, 1015, 1160) yd/
795 (795, 928, 928, 1061) m of DK weight yarn, 100% baby alpaca, in natural

Needles

3.5 mm (size 4 U.S.) circular, 24"/61 cm or 32"/81 cm long
or size to obtain correct gauge

Notions

Snap tape, ½ yd/46 cm
Tapestry needle

GAUGE

21 sts and 30 rows = 4"/
10.2 cm in St st

Always take time to check your gauge.

THIS PROJECT WAS KNIT WITH:

Fable Handknits Baby Alpaca
(100% baby alpaca; 145 yd/50 g):
6 (6, 7, 7, 8) skeins, Natural (06)

PATTERN NOTES

The upper and lower pieces are joined using a technique commonly used to attach an edging to the main body of a lace shawl. In this seamless method, you work together one live, held st from one piece with one st of the piece you are working on.

RS Row: Slip the last stitch from the upper piece knitwise, slip the next stitch from the lower piece knitwise, knit together (like a ssk).

WS Row: Purl together the last stitch of the upper piece with the next stitch on the lower piece.

INSTRUCTIONS

Lower Body

With provisional or invisible cast on and waste yarn, CO 158 (168, 178, 188, 198) sts.

Working rows back and forth, work picot edging as follows.

Rows 1–5: Beg with a p row, work 5 rows in St st.

Row 6: K1, (k2tog, yo) to last st, k1.

Rows 7–11: Beg and end with a p row, work 5 rows in St st.

Row 12: Fold hem over so the CO edge is aligned with the last row worked. K tog 1 st from the provisional CO (looks like a purl bump) with a st on your needle. Remove waste yarn.

Next, work 4 (5, 5, 5, 6) rows even. Pm 4 times for dart shaping as follows: work 24 (25, 26, 27, 28) sts, pm; work 35 (38, 41, 44, 47) sts, pm; work 40 (42, 44, 46, 48) sts, pm; work 35 (38, 42, 44, 47) st, pm; work last 24 (25, 25, 27, 28) sts.

WAIST DECREASES

Dec Row: K to 1st marker, sm, k2tog, k to 2 sts before 2nd marker, ssk, sm, k to 3rd marker, sm, k2tog, k to 2 sts before 4th m, ssk, sm, k to end—4 decs.

Work a dec row every 6 rows 5 times total—138 (148, 158, 168, 178) st rem.

Cont to work even until piece measures 4½ (5, 5, 5, 5½)"/11.4 (12.7, 12.7, 12.7, 14) cm from hem edge.

BUST SHAPING

Inc Row: K to 1st m, sm, m1l, knit to the 2nd m, m1r, sm, k to the 3rd m, sm, m1l, k to the 4th m, m1r, sm, k to end.

Work an inc row every 8 (8, 10, 10, 10) rows 5 times total—158 (168, 178, 188, 198) st rem.

Cont to work even until piece measures 10 (11, 11½, 12, 13)"/ 25.4(27.9, 29.2, 30.5, 33) cm from CO edge.

Place all sts on waste yarn or a spare circular needle.

Sms 0 (3, 4, 4, 4) sts from either side of the back darts ms to help align pieces when attaching.

Sms 42 (44, 46, 49, 51) sts from each edge to indicate the side "seams."

UPPER BODY, LEFT SIDE

With provisional or invisible cast on, waste yarn, and circular needles, CO 60 (63, 66, 69, 72) sts.

Working back and forth, work picot edge as for Lower Body hem.
P 1 row even.

Begin short row shaping as follows.

Row 1: K3, w/t.

Row 2 (and all WS rows): P to the last st, p the last st with 1 st of the Lower Body. This will attach the upper piece to the lower piece of the cardigan.

Row 3 (RS): K to the wrapped st, p/u wrap, and k the st and its wrap tog, k2, w/t.

Cont rows 2 and 3 until all 60 (63, 66, 69, 72) sts have been worked and 20, 21, 22, 23, 24 sts have been worked from Lower Body.

At the end of the last RS row, provisionally CO 47 (50, 53, 56, 59) sts for the back—107 (113, 119, 125, 131) sts total.

Work even in St st and AT THE SAME TIME, beg at the left side m, attach the Upper Body to the Lower Body as follows: K to the last st, sl the last st kwise, sl a st from the Lower Body kwise, k the 2 sts tog tbl as for ssk

Cont until 10 (12, 14, 16, 18) sts rem on lower body piece.

Attaching Upper to Lower Body on the Front

P to the last st, ptog the last st with 2 sts from the lower body.

DIRECTION OF KNITTING FOR RETRO PICOT

STEP 1

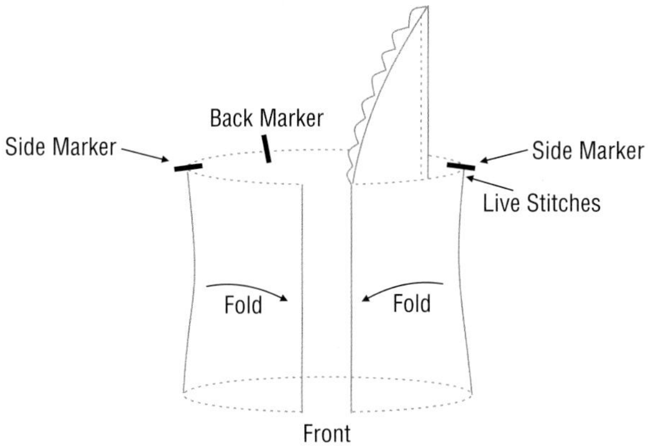
Back Marker
Side Marker
Side Marker
Live Stitches
Fold
Fold
Front

STEP 2

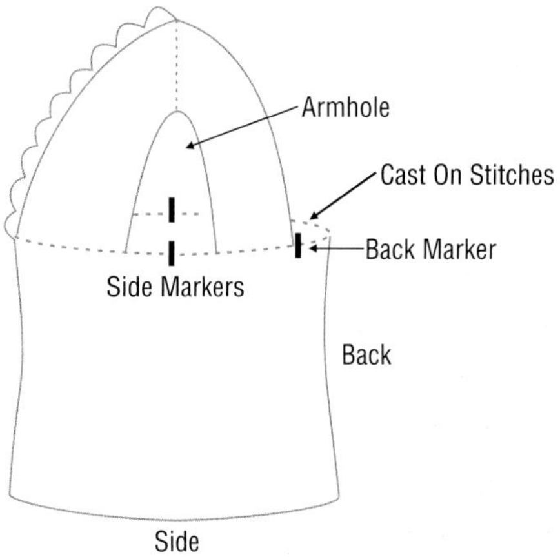
Armhole
Cast On Stitches
Back Marker
Side Markers
Back
Side

STEP 3

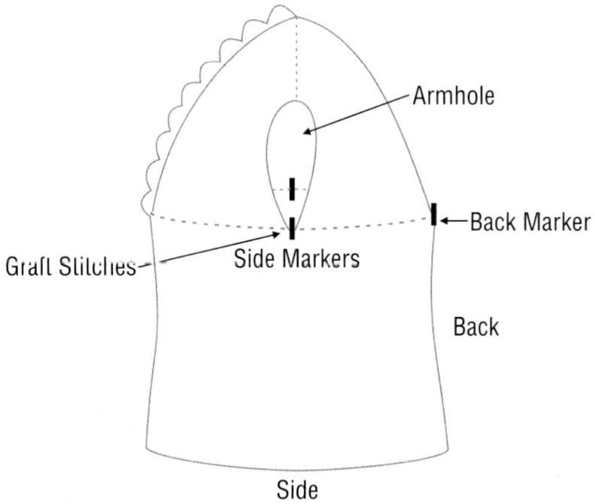
Armhole
Back Marker
Graft Stitches
Side Markers
Back
Side

STEP 4

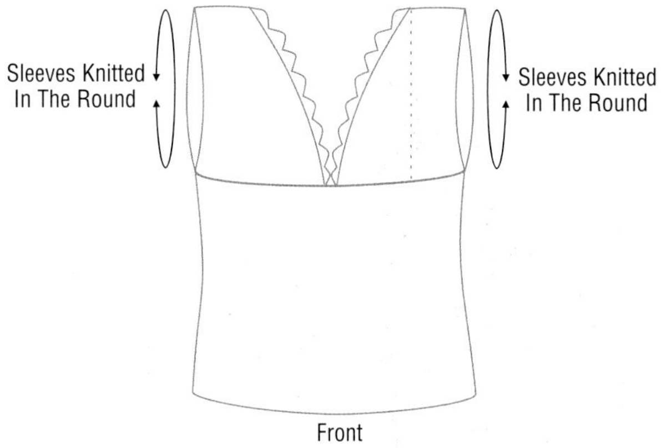
Sleeves Knitted
In The Round
Sleeves Knitted
In The Round
Front

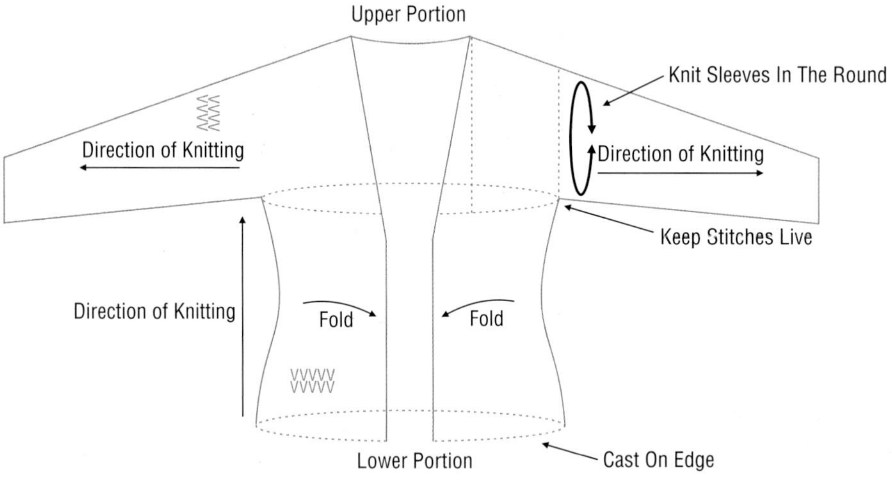
Upper Portion
Knit Sleeves In The Round
Direction of Knitting
Direction of Knitting
Keep Stitches Live
Direction of Knitting
Fold
Fold
Lower Portion
Cast On Edge

Attaching Upper Body to Lower Body on the Back

K to the last st, sl the last st kwise, sl2 sts kwise from the Lower Body, and k3tog as for ssk.

Cont until all sts from the lower piece are attached to the Left Front.

SLEEVES

Join to work in the rnd.

Row 1: K to the last 5 (5, 6, 7, 8) sts on the back, and place those sts on waste yarn. Then, place the first 5 (5, 6, 7, 8) sts of the row on waste yarn—97 (103, 107, 111, 115) sts.

Row 2: Rep row 1—87, (93, 95, 97, 99) sts rem.

Row 3: K to the last 8 sts of the back, and place those 8 sts on waste yarn. Then, place the first 8 sts of the row on waste yarn—71 (77, 79, 81, 83) sts rem.

SLEEVE DECREASES

Pm at the underseam.

Dec Row: K2, ssk, k to last 4 st, k2tog, k2—2 sts dec.

Work the decrease row every 6 (6, 7, 7, 8) rows, 8 times total—55 (61, 63, 65, 67) st rem.

Work in St st to desired length, and then work a picot edging as follows.

Row 1: *K2tog, yo, rep from * to end.

Rows 2–6: Work 5 rows even. Place sts on waste yarn.

Fold hem to inside along picot line, and sew each st to the inside.

UPPER BODY, RIGHT SIDE

Remove waste yarn from the provisional CO and place all sts on the needle. You will have one less st than what you had provisionally CO—46 (49, 52, 55, 58) sts. Pick up one st close to the lower piece—47 (50, 53, 56, 59) sts total. Work the Upper Back even, in St st, and attach the Lower Back to the Upper Back piece as you go along, until you reach the back marker on the right side. Place all sts on waste yarn or a spare circular needle. Break yarn.

Neck

Work the V-neck as follows: With provisional or invisible cast on and waste yarn, CO 60 (63, 66, 69, 72) st. Work picot edge.

Begin short rows as follows: P3, wrap the next st, and turn.

Next row (and all RS rows): K to the last st, sl last st kwise, sl a st of the lower piece kwise, k them tog as for ssk. This will attach the Upper Right Front to the Lower Right Front of the cardigan.

RS: P to the wrapped st, pick up wrap, and p tog the st with its wrap, p2, w/t.

Cont until all 60 (63, 66, 69, 72) st have been worked—20, 21, 22, 23, 24 sts picked up from lower piece.

Join the 60 (63, 66, 69, 72) sts of the Right Front and the 47 (50, 53, 56, 59) sts of the Right Back in the rnd—107 (113, 119, 125, 131) sts total. Note that you will now work the Right Upper Front and the Right Upper Back as one piece.

Cont until 10 (12, 14, 16, 18) sts rem on the lower body.

Attaching the Upper Back Body to the Lower Back

P to the last st, p tog the last st and 2 sts from the lower body.

Attaching the Upper Front Body to the Lower Front

K to the last st, sl the last st kwise, sl2 sts from the lower body, and k3 tog tbl as for ssk.

Cont until all sts from the Lower Body are attached to the Upper Body.
Remove "side seam" marker.
Work sleeve as for left side.

EDGING

Row 1: P/u 1 st in each row along the left edge, from top to bottom.

Row 2: *P2, p2tog, rep from * to end.

Rows 3–6: Work even in St st.

Row 7: *K2tog, yo, rep from * to end.

Rows 8–12: Work even in St st.
Place all sts on waste yarn.

Fold hem to inside along picot and sew each st to the inside.

FINISHING

Rep rows 1–12 on left edge.
P/u sts along the back neck, 1 st per row. Work rows 1–12 as for left edge.

Sew in snap tape on underside of both front edges, placing flat part of snap on left side.

Weave in ends. Graft together the live sts at underarm. Block.

RETRO PICOT SCHEMATIC

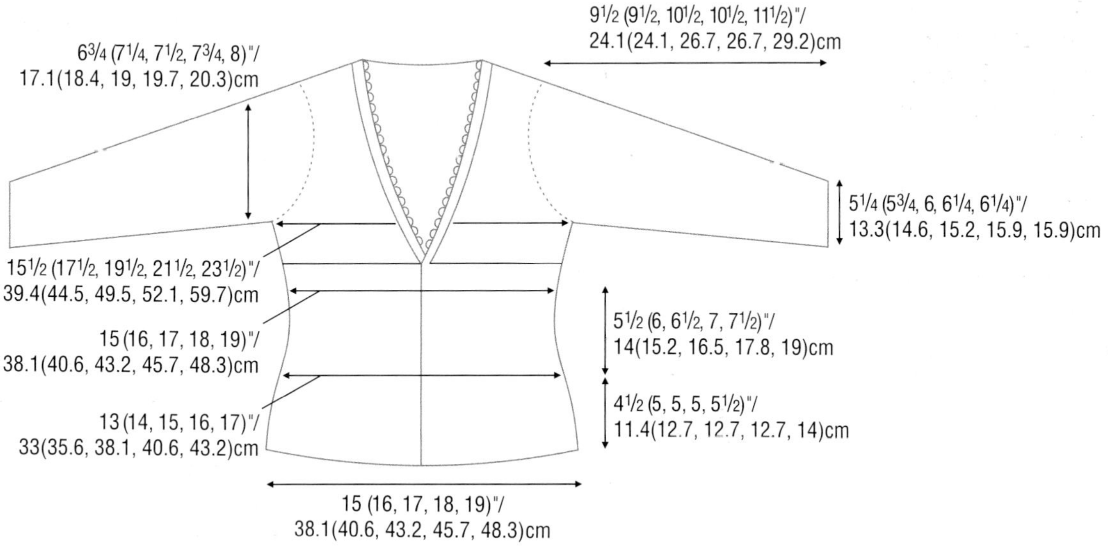
6 3/4 (7 1/4, 7 1/2, 7 3/4, 8)"/
17.1(18.4, 19, 19.7, 20.3)cm
9 1/2 (9 1/2, 10 1/2, 10 1/2, 11 1/2)"/
24.1(24.1, 26.7, 26.7, 29.2)cm
5 1/4 (5 3/4, 6, 6 1/4, 6 1/4)"/
13.3(14.6, 15.2, 15.9, 15.9)cm
15 1/2 (17 1/2, 19 1/2, 21 1/2, 23 1/2)"/
39.4(44.5, 49.5, 52.1, 59.7)cm
15 (16, 17, 18, 19)"/
38.1(40.6, 43.2, 45.7, 48.3)cm
5 1/2 (6, 6 1/2, 7, 7 1/2)"/
14(15.2, 16.5, 17.8, 19)cm
13 (14, 15, 16, 17)"/
33(35.6, 38.1, 40.6, 43.2)cm
4 1/2 (5, 5, 5, 5 1/2)"/
11.4(12.7, 12.7, 12.7, 14)cm
15 (16, 17, 18, 19)"/
38.1(40.6, 43.2, 45.7, 48.3)cm

DIMPLE V-NECK

LUCINDA SNYDER

This classic piece will add a subtle elegance to your wardrobe. The sheen and drape of the silk and alpaca yarns are used in different shades and textures. It can be worn by itself or with a camisole underneath. Play with the color combination to dress it up or down.

THIS PROJECT WAS KNIT WITH:

Yarn A: Blue Sky Silk and Alpaca (50% alpaca, 50% silk, 146 yd/50 g): 6 (7, 7, 8, 9) skeins, White

Yarn B: Blue Sky Silk and Alpaca (50% alpaca, 50% silk, 146 yd/50 g): 2 (2, 3, 4, 4) skeins, Ecru

PATTERN NOTES

Work a selvedge stitch on each edge of all pieces. Selvedge sts are included in the total stitch count. It may be helpful to place a marker after the first stitch and before the last stitch.

Unless otherwise noted, all decreases are worked as follows: ssk or k2tog 2 or 3 sts from the edge.

PATTERN STITCHES

Dimple Stitch

Multiple of 2 sts.

Row 1: *K1, sl1 kwise; repeat from * to the end.

Row 2: Sl the slips pwise and p the purls.

Row 3: K.

Row 4: P.

Row 5: *Sl1 kwise, k1; repeat from * to the end.

Row 6: Rep row 2.

Row 7: K.

Row 8: P.

SELVEDGE STITCH

Row 1: Sl first st kwise, work across row, p the last st.

INSTRUCTIONS

BACK

Using Yarn A and 3.75 mm needles, CO 106 (112, 118, 124, 134) sts. Work even in St st for 1"/ 2.5 cm. On the next RS row, dec 1 st at each end rep every 7 rows 7 times total—92 (98, 104, 110, 120) sts rem.

Work even until piece measures 8"/20.3 cm from the CO edge or desired length.

Change to 3.5 mm needles and Yarn B, and work even in St st for 2 rows. Change to Dimple Stitch patt and work for 3"/7.6 cm.

Change back to 3.75 mm needles and Yarn A, and work even in St st for 5"/12.7 cm.

SKILL LEVEL

Easy

SIZES

XS (S, M, L, XL)
34 (36, 38, 40, 42)"/
86 (91, 97, 102, 107) cm
Shown in size XS

FINISHED MEASUREMENTS

Chest: 34 (36, 38, 40, 42)"/
86 (91, 97, 102, 107) cm
Length: 24"/61 cm
Sleeve: 20"/51 cm

MATERIALS AND TOOLS

Yarn

Color A: 876 (1022, 1022, 1168, 1314) yd/801 (935, 935 1068, 1202) m of sport weight yarn, 50% alpaca, 50% silk, in white

Color B: 292 (292, 438, 584, 584) yd/267 (267, 401, 534, 534) m of sport weight yarn, 50% alpaca, 50% silk, in ecru

Needles

3.5 mm (size 4 U.S.) straight
3.75 mm (size 5 U.S.) straight
or size to obtain correct gauge

Notions

Crochet hook

GAUGE

22 sts and 28 rows = 4"/10.2 cm in St st on 3.75 mm needles
28 sts and 42 rows = 4"/10.2 cm in Dimple Stitch on 3.5 mm needles

Always take time to check your gauge.

Shape Armhole

BO 5 sts at the beg of the next 2 rows—82 (88, 94, 100, 110) sts rem.

BO 3 sts at the beg of the next 2 rows—76 (82, 88, 94, 104) sts rem.

Dec 1 st at each end every other row on the RS 4 times—68 (74, 80, 86, 96) sts rem.

Work even until armhole measures 7½"/19 cm.

Shape Shoulder

BO 7 sts at the beg of the next 4 rows—40 (46, 52, 58, 68) sts rem.

BO the remaining 40 (46, 52, 58, 68) sts for the back of the neck.

FRONT

Work as for Back through completion of the Dimple Stitch section.

Divide for V-neck

Working each side separately, k46 (49, 52, 55, 60) sts, attach new ball of yarn, and k46 (49, 52, 55, 60) sts. P 1 row. Continue working both sides at the same time, reversing shaping.

Dec 1 st at neck edge every other row on RS row 23 times.

When work measures 5"/12.7 cm above Dimple Stitch section, beg shaping each armhole AT THE SAME TIME you continue neck shaping.

Shape Armhole

At the beg of the next RS row, BO 5 sts.

Then, BO 3 sts at the beg of the next RS row.

Dec 1 st at the beg of every RS row 3 times.

Work even until armhole measures 7½"/19 cm.

Shape Shoulder

BO 6 (7, 7, 7, 7) sts at the beg of the next 2 RS rows for all sizes.

BO remaining 0 (0, 3, 6, 11) sts.

SLEEVES (Make 2)

With 3.5 mm needles and Yarn B, CO 72 (72, 77, 82, 82) sts.

Work in St st for 2 rows, and then work in Dimple Stitch for 5"/12.7.

Change to 3.75 mm needles and Yarn A, and work even in St st until piece measures 20"/51 cm from the CO edge.

Shape Cap

BO 5 sts at the beg of the next 2 rows—62 (62, 67, 72, 72) sts rem.

BO 3 sts at the beg of the next 2 rows—56 (56, 61, 66, 66) sts rem.

Dec 1 st at each side every other row on the RS 12 times—32 (32, 37, 42, 42) sts rem.

Then, BO 4 (4, 5, 5, 5) sts at the beg of the next 4 rows—16 (16, 17, 22, 22) sts rem.

BO remaining 16 (16, 17, 22, 22) sts.

FINISHING

Block all pieces. Sew Back and Front together at shoulder seams. Sew sleeves into armholes. Sew side seams and sleeves in one continuous seam.

Using Yarn A, single crochet around front and back bottom edges, and around neckline and bottom of sleeves.

DIMPLE V-NECK SCHEMATIC

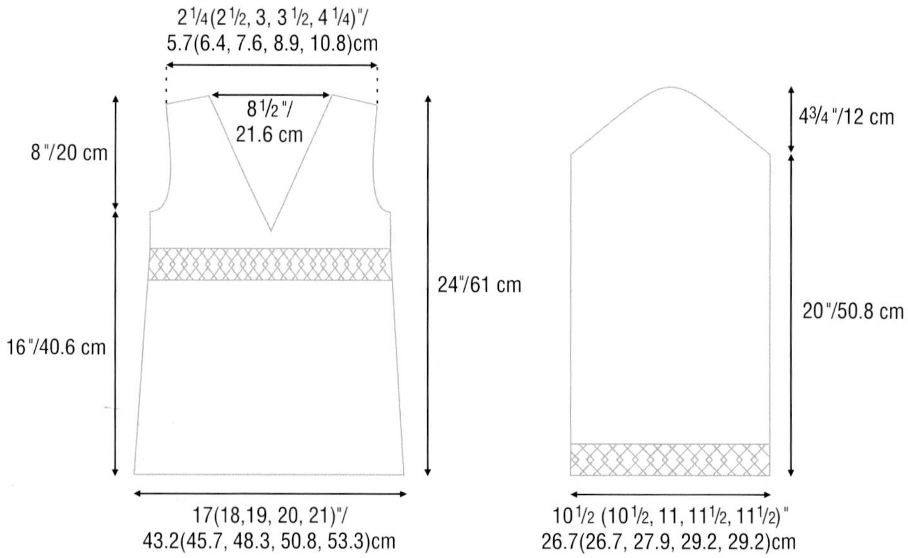
2 1/4(2 1/2, 3, 3 1/2, 4 1/4)"/
5.7(6.4, 7.6, 8.9, 10.8)cm
8 1/2"/
21.6 cm
8"/20 cm
16"/40.6 cm
24"/61 cm
17(18,19, 20, 21)"/
43.2(45.7, 48.3, 50.8, 53.3)cm
4 3/4"/12 cm
20"/50.8 cm
10 1/2 (10 1/2, 11, 11 1/2, 11 1/2)"
26.7(26.7, 27.9, 29.2, 29.2)cm

LUXURY CLOCHE

ILLANNA WEINER

Pamper your head with a simple cashmere cloche. This lovely hat features a beautiful starburst design on the crown and a crisp fold-under brim. The buttery soft cashmere yarn provides ultimate luxury, while the small needles create a dense and sturdy knit. The inspiration for the Luxury Cloche comes from gardening in New York City, with memories of bundling up and planting tulip bulbs in December and anticipating the spring blooms.

SKILL LEVEL

Intermediate

SIZES

S (M)
20 (22)"/51 (55) cm
Shown in size S

FINISHED MEASUREMENTS

Head circumference:
20 (22)"/51 (55) cm

MATERIALS AND TOOLS

Yarn

246 (328) yd/225 (300) m
of chunky weight yarn,
100% cashmere, in white

Needles

4.0 mm (size 6 U.S.) circular,
16"/41 cm long
4.0 mm (size 6 U.S.) dpns
or size to obtain correct gauge

Notions

Tapestry needle
6.0 mm (size J U.S.) crochet hook
Removable stitch marker
Smooth waste yarn in a
contrasting color

GAUGE

22 sts and 28 rows = 4"/
10.2 cm in St st

Always take time to check your gauge.

THIS PROJECT WAS KNIT WITH:

Laines Du Nord "Royal Cashmere" (100% Cashmere; 82 yd/25 g): 3 (4) balls, white (1)

PATTERN NOTES

The Luxury Cloche is knit seamlessly from the top down, beginning with a provisional cast on. The increases form a lovely swirl at the crown. The brim is folded over and seamed to create a clean edge.

Begin with double pointed needles and change to the circular needle when the stitches comfortably fit without stretching.

To substitute yarns: The recommended yarn gauge for heavyweight yarn of this type is 14 sts = 4"/10.2 cm in St st on 6.0 mm (size 10 U.S.) needles, but this pattern is knit tightly on 4.0 mm (size 6 U.S.) needles to create a sturdier, denser fabric.

INSTRUCTIONS

Using waste yarn and 6.0 mm (size J) crochet hook, chain 10. Leaving a 12"/31 cm-long tail, with one dpn, pick up and k6 sts evenly spaced in the back loops of the crochet chain. Divide sts on 3 dpns. Join to knit in the rnd, placing a removable marker in the first st.

Rnd 1 (and all odd number rows): K.

Rnd 2: *K1, m1, pm,* rep between * around. You should have a total of 6 markers.

Rnd 4 (and all even number rows): *K to m, m1, slip m,* repeat between * around.

Repeat rnds 3–4 until you have 108 (120) sts on the needle and 18 (19) sts between markers (16 rnds), changing to circular needle when piece is large enough.

Work even in St st until piece measures 3"/7.6 cm from end of incs.

Begin brim shaping as follows:

Rnd 1: *K to m, m1,* repeat between * around.

Rnds 2–5: K.

Rnd 6: Repeat rnd 1.

Rnds 7–10: K.

Rnd 11: P.

Rnds 12–15: K.

Rnd 16: *K to 2 sts before m, k2tog,* rep between * around.

Rnds 17–20: K.

Rnd 21: Repeat rnd 16.

Rnds 22–24: K.

BO all sts. Break the yarn, leaving a 30"/76 cm-long tail.

FINISHING

Remove waste yarn from provisional CO, placing the 6 sts on dpns. Thread the CO tail onto a tapestry needle and pull it through the 6 sts. Pull the tail to the inside of the hat.

Fold brim to wrong side along purl ridge. Using the tail and tapestry needle, invisibly sew the BO edge to the inside of the hat.

Block piece and pin to correct measurements. Weave in all ends.

BABY CARDIGAN WITH SCARF

CONNIE CHANG CHINCHIO

This simple yet sweet baby cardigan is worked in super-soft yak down in one piece. A slipped-stitch, yarn-over ridge edges the cardigan and is worked as subtle stripes in the attached scarf. Garter stitch bands make a casual edging, and pom-poms grace the ends of the scarf, lending a playful touch to a basic winter cardi.

THIS PROJECT WAS KNIT WITH:

Shokay Pure Yak Down
(100% Yak Down; 164 yd/100 g):
2 (3, 3, 4) skeins, Alpine

PATTERN NOTES

The first and last stitches are worked in garter stitch for easier seaming.

PATTERN STITCHES

RIDGE PATTERN

Multiple of 3 sts

Row 1 (WS): K1, *wyif sl1 pwise, yo; rep from * to last st, k1.

Row 2 (RS): K1, *ktog tbl slipped st and yo; rep from * to last st, k1.

Row 3 (WS): K1, p to last st, k1.

Row 4 (RS): K.

Row 5 (WS): Rep row 3.

Row 6 (RS): K.

MODESITT SLIP STITCH EDGING

Row 1 (RS): K1, sl1 wyif, k1, work center sts in desired pattern to last 3 sts, k1, sl1 wyif, k1.

Row 2 (WS): Sl1 wyif, k1, sl1 wyif, work center sts in desired pattern to last 3 sts, sl1 wyif, k1, sl1 wyif.

INSTRUCTIONS

Body

With 4.5 mm needles, CO 82 (92, 99, 111) sts. Work 2 rows garter st. Change to 5.0 mm needles and St st.

Next row (RS): K20 (22, 24, 27), pm, k42 (48, 51, 57), pm, k20 (22, 24, 27). Work even in St st for 4 more rows, ending with a WS row.

Work rows 1–6 of the Ridge patt, then work rows 1–2 of the Ridge patt.

Cont working even in St st until piece measures 5¾ (6¼, 7½, 8½)"/14.6 (15.8, 19, 21.6) cm from CO edge, ending with a WS row.

Divide for Front and Back

Next row: K to 3 sts before 1st m, BO 3 sts, remove m, BO 3 sts, k to 3 sts before 2nd m, BO 3 sts, remove m, BO 3 sts, k to end—70 (80, 87, 99) sts rem.

SKILL LEVEL

Intermediate

SIZES

6 (9, 12, 18) months
Shown in size 18 months

FINISHED MEASUREMENTS

Chest circumference: 18½ (20½, 22½, 25)"/47 (52, 57, 64) cm
Length: 10 (11, 12½, 14)"/ 25 (28, 32, 36) cm
Sleeve length: 6 (6¾, 7½, 8¾)"/15.2 (17.1, 19, 22.2) cm
Neck width: 5¼ (5¾, 6, 6½)"/ 13.3 (14.6, 15.2, 16.5) cm

MATERIALS AND TOOLS

Yarn

328 (492, 492, 656) yd/300 (450, 450, 600) m of worsted weight yarn, 100% Yak Down, in alpine

Needles

5.0 mm (size 8 U.S.) circular, 24"/61 cm or 32"/81 cm long
4.5 mm (size 7 U.S.) circular, 24"/61 cm or 32"/81 cm long
or size to obtain correct gauge

Notions

Stitch markers
Stitch holders
Darning needles

GAUGE

18 sts and 24 rows = 4"/10.2 cm in St st on 5.0 mm needles

Always take time to check your gauge.

SAFETY NOTE:

Keep your little one safe and in sight, if you opt to tie the scarf.

Left Front

Cont to work in St st until armhole depth measures 2¾ (3¼, 3½, 4)"/ 6.9 (8.2, 8.9, 10.2) cm, ending with a RS row.

Neck Shaping

Cont working in St st, working even on the RS rows and BO at beg of WS rows as follows.

6 (6, 6, 7) sts 1 time.

3 (4, 4, 4) sts 1 time.

1 st 2 times.

Work even until armhole depth measures 4¼ (4¾, 5, 5½)"/10.8 (12.1, 12.7, 14) cm.

Leave rem 6 (7, 9, 11) sts on holder for left shoulder.

Right Front

Attach yarn at armhole edge of the right front.

Work as for left front, reversing all shaping.

Back

Attach yarn at left armhole edge, ready to begin a WS row.

Work even in St st until piece measures 9½ (10½, 12, 13½)"/24 (27, 31, 34) cm from CO edge, ending with a WS row.

Next row (RS): K7 (8, 10, 12), BO 24 (26, 27, 29), k7 (8, 10, 12).

Attach yarn to the neck edge of the right half piece and work both sides at the same time as follows.

Next row (WS): P.
Place rem 6 (7, 9, 11) sts of each back shoulder on st holders.

SLEEVES (Make 2)

With 4.5 mm needles, CO 26 (28, 32, 34) sts.

Work 2 rows in garter stitch.

Change to 5.0 mm needles and work 4 rows in St st.

Inc row (RS): K1, m1l, knit to last two sts, m1r, k1.

Work rows 1–6 of Ridge patt, then rows 1–2 of Ridge patt.

Next row (WS): K1, p to last st, k1.

Next row (RS): Rep inc row every 5 (5, 6, 6) rows 4 (5, 5, 6) times more—36 (40, 44, 48) sts.

Work even until sleeve measures 6 (6¾, 7½, 8¾)"/15.2 (17.1, 19, 22.2) cm from CO edge.

Work even for 4 rows. BO all sts.

SCARF

With 4.5 mm needles, CO 12 sts.
Note: Maintain Modesitt's Slip Stitch Edging on the first 3 and last 3 sts.

Work 2 rows in garter st.

Change to 5.0 mm needles.

Work 3 rows in St st.

Work in Ridge patt until the scarf measures 4 (5, 6½, 8)"/10.2 (12.7, 16.5, 20.3) cm, ending with a WS row.

Next row (RS): Continue to work Modesitt's Slip Stitch Edging on the first 3 sts, work to the last 3 sts, k2tog, k1—11 sts rem.

Next row (WS): K1, work to the last 3 sts, work Modesitt's Slip Stitch Edging. Rep last 2 rows in Ridge patt until this section of the scarf is equal in length to the back neck width plus 2"/5 cm.

Next row (RS): Work to last 2 sts, m1, sl1, k1—12 sts rem.

Resume working Modesitt's Slip Stitch Edging on both sides of the scarf, and cont working in Ridge patt for another 4 (5, 6½, 8)"/10.2 (12.7, 16.5, 20.3) cm.

FINISHING

Seam shoulders using 3-needle BO. Sew sleeves to armholes, lining up the last 4 rows of the sleeve with the 3-stitch BO indentation in the armhole.

Sew sleeve seams.

With RS out, sew the garter st edge of scarf to the back neck and front neck, stopping at the BO sts.

Front Bands

With 4.5 mm needles and RS facing, p/u 23 (27, 34, 41) sts along right front, p/u 9 (10, 10, 11) sts along the right front neck edge, stopping where the scarf is attached.

Work 2 rows garter st.

BO kwise.

Repeat for left front band, beginning to pick up sts on neck edge.

Sew right front neck edging to right front. Rep for left.

BABY CARDIGAN WITH SCARF SCHEMATIC

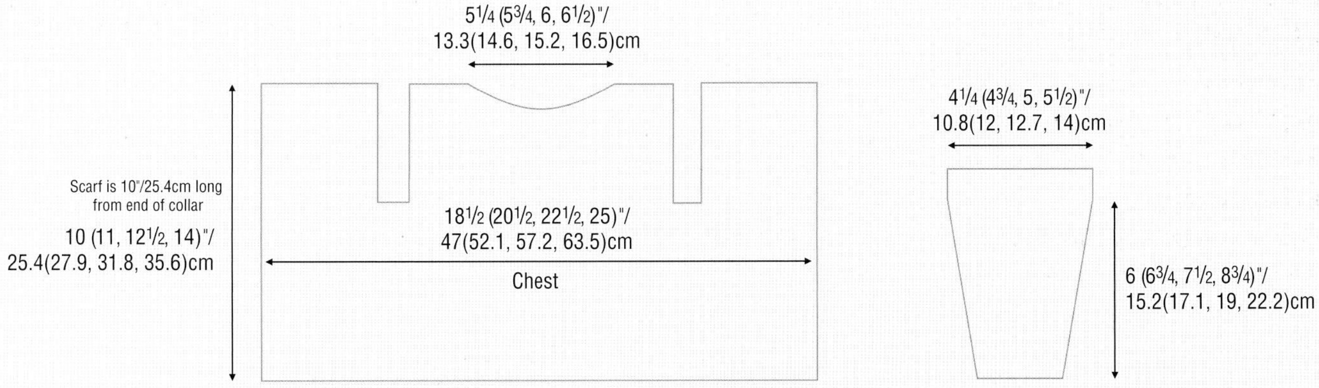
5¼ (5¾, 6, 6½)"/
13.3(14.6, 15.2, 16.5)cm
Scarf is 10"/25.4cm long from end of collar
10 (11, 12½, 14)"/
25.4(27.9, 31.8, 35.6)cm
18½ (20½, 22½, 25)"/
47(52.1, 57.2, 63.5)cm
Chest
4¼ (4¾, 5, 5½)"/
10.8(12, 12.7, 14)cm
6 (6¾, 7½, 8¾)"/
15.2(17.1, 19, 22.2)cm

PINTUCK PANEL

KALANI CRAIG

This could be called the *Pure Knits* "official uniform." With its modern styling, graceful neckline, and sexy, sheer panel, what's not to love? Diagonal pintucks slant downward to a center-attached I-cord in this uniquely sophisticated piece that reflects the hallmarks of the collection.

SKILL LEVEL

Intermediate

SIZES

XS (S, M, L, XL, 2X, 3X, 4X, 5X)
30 (34, 38, 42, 47, 51, 55, 59, 64)"/76 (86, 97, 102, 119, 130, 140, 150, 163) cm
Shown in size S

FINISHED MEASUREMENTS

Bust: 31 (35, 39½, 43½, 48, 52, 56½, 60½, 65)"/79 (89, 100, 110, 122, 132, 144, 154, 169) cm
Length, armhole to hip: 13¼ (13½, 14, 14½, 15, 15½, 16, 16½, 17)"/34 (34, 36, 37, 38, 39, 41, 42, 43) cm
Width at hem: 15½ (17½, 19¾, 21¾, 24, 26, 28¼, 30¼, 32½)"/39 (45, 50, 55, 61, 66, 72, 77, 83) cm
Sleeve width: 12 (12½, 13½, 15, 16½, 17¾, 19½, 21¾, 23½)"/31 (32, 34, 38, 42, 45, 50, 55, 60) cm

MATERIALS AND TOOLS

Yarn

Color A: 764 (764, 995, 995, 1146, 1337, 1337, 1528, 1528) yd/699 (699, 910, 910, 1048, 1223, 1223, 1397, 1397) m of fingering weight yarn, 100% superwash merino wool, in natural
Color B: 330 (330, 660, 660, 660, 660, 660, 660, 990) yd/302 (302, 604, 604, 604, 604, 604, 604, 905) m of lace weight yarn, 60% kid mohair, 40% silk, in ivory

Needles

2.75 mm (size 2 U.S.) straight
3.5 mm (size 4 U.S.) straight
3.5 mm (size 4 U.S.) dpns
4.0 mm (size 6 U.S.) straight
or size to obtain correct gauge

GAUGE

26 sts and 38 rows = 4"/10.2 cm in Yarn A on 2.75 mm needles
22 sts and 26 rows = 4"/10.2 cm in Yarn B on 3.5 mm needles

Always take time to check your gauge.

THIS PROJECT WAS KNIT WITH:

Yarn A: ShibuiKnits Sock
(100% superwash merino wool; 191 yd/50 g): 4 (4, 5, 5, 6, 7, 7, 8, 8) skeins, Natural

Yarn B: ShibuiKnits Silk Cloud
(60% kid mohair, 40% silk; 330 yd/25 g): 1 (1, 2, 2, 2, 2, 2, 2, 3) skeins, Ivory (SC7501)

PATTERN NOTES

Waist shaping increases are worked 2 sts from the edge using m1l and m1rs. Kfb/pfb increases were used at the base triangle.

Waist and armhole shapings are as follows.

INCREASES

(RS) K2, m1l, work to 2 sts before end, m1r, k2.

(WS) P2, m1pl, work to 2 sts before end, m1pr, p2.

DECREASES

(RS) K1, ssk, work to 3 sts before end, k2tog, k1.

(WS) P1, p2tog, work to 3 sts before end, ssp, p1.

SPECIAL ABBREVIATIONS

m1pr (make one purl right): p/u bar between sts from back, purl through front

m1pl (make one purl left): p/u bar between sts from front, purl through back

INSTRUCTIONS

Back

Using invisible or provisional cast-on, scrap yarn, and 4.0 mm needles, CO 52 (58, 65, 72, 79, 86, 93, 100, 107) sts. Change to Yarn B and work 6 rows in St st, ending with a WS row. Change to 2.75 mm needles and kfb into each st for a total of 104 (116, 130, 144, 158, 172, 186, 200, 214) sts.

Change to Yarn A and begin waist shaping on next page.

SHAPING

Work 6 (6, 6, 7, 8, 8, 9, 9, 10) rows. Dec 1 st each seam next row. Rep between * 8 (8, 8, 8, 7, 7, 7, 7, 7) times—88 (100, 114, 128, 144, 158, 172, 186, 200) sts.

AT THE SAME TIME, after 7 rows, work every other st tog with sts from provisional CO to create a folded hem, adjusting to accommodate waist decs. Remove scrap yarn.

Work even for 6 (8, 5, 2, 10, 14, 5, 10, 8) rows.

Work 7 (7, 8, 8, 9, 9, 10, 10, 10) rows. Inc 1 st each seam next row. Rep between * 8 (8, 8, 8, 7, 7, 7, 7, 7) times—104 (116, 130, 144, 158, 172, 186, 200, 214) sts.

Armhole Shaping

BO 6 (6, 6, 8, 8, 11, 11, 13, 13) sts at beg of next 2 rows.

Dec 1 st each side every row 2 (2, 2, 2, 3, 2, 3, 3, 3) times.

Dec 1 st each side every other row on RS row 5 (7, 8, 8, 9, 8, 9, 8, 10) times.

Work even for 58 (54, 59, 66, 65, 76, 75, 84, 87) rows—78 (86, 98,108,118, 130, 140, 152,162) sts.

Place rem sts on st holder.

FRONT OUTSIDE PANEL
(Make 2)

Using invisible or provisional cast-on, scrap yarn, and 4.0 mm needles, CO 17 (19, 22, 24, 26, 29, 31, 33, 36) sts.

Change to Yarn B and work 6 rows in St st, ending with a WS row. Change to 2.75 mm needles and kfb into each st for a total of 34 (38, 44, 48, 52, 58, 62, 66, 72) sts.

Change to Yarn A and begin shaping on one side as for back, reversing shaping on second panel. AT THE SAME TIME, after 7 rows, work every other st together with sts from provisional CO to create a folded hem, adjusting to accommodate waist decs. Continue working waist and armhole shaping as for back—21 (23, 28, 30, 32, 37, 39, 42, 46) sts.

Place rem sts on st holder.

FRONT CENTER PANEL

Base Triangle (Make 2)

Using Yarn B and 3.5 mm dpns, CO 3 sts. Working in St st, *inc 1 st each side next 3 rows, work even 1 row.* Rep between * until there are 24 (28, 31, 34, 38, 40, 43, 47, 50) sts. Put aside and rep with other two dpns.

Arrange both base triangles so RS faces and CO tails are on the outside bottom corners.

Starting with right triangle, k to end of first base triangle, pm, CO 4 sts, join second triangle, pm, and work to end.

Pintucks

Work 2 (2, 2, 2, 2, 2, 2, 2, 2) rows straight. Mark row to be tucked by weaving scrap yarn in and out of stitches of row immediately below needle. Work even for 4 (4, 4, 4, 4, 4, 4, 4, 4) rows, ending with a WS row. Fold up marked row and k those sts together with sts on needle to create pintuck.

Work next 14 (14, 14, 16, 16, 16, 18, 18, 18) rows while working shaping rows on all RS rows and on every other WS row at markers as follows.

RS Shaping Row: Kfb, work 20 (24, 27, 30, 34, 36, 39, 43, 46), k2tog, k4, ssk, work to last st, kfb.

WS Shaping Row: Pfb, work 20 (24, 27, 30, 34, 36, 39, 43, 46), ssp, p4, p2tog, work to last st, pfb.

End with a WS row.

Work pintuck and shaping a total of 5 times. Remove scrap yarn. Place sts on waste yarn.

SLEEVE (Make 2)

Using invisible or provisional cast-on, scrap yarn, and 4.0 mm needles, CO 39 (41, 44, 49, 53, 58, 63, 71, 76) sts.

Work 4 rows in St st, ending with a WS row. Change to 2.75 mm needles. Kfb into each st for a total of 78 (82, 88, 98, 106, 116, 126, 142, 152) sts.

Change to Yarn A and work 4 rows in St st. On 5th row, work every other st tog with sts from provisional CO to create a folded hem, adjusting to accommodate decs. Remove scrap yarn.

Begin shaping as follows, on next page.

PINTUCK PANEL SCHEMATIC

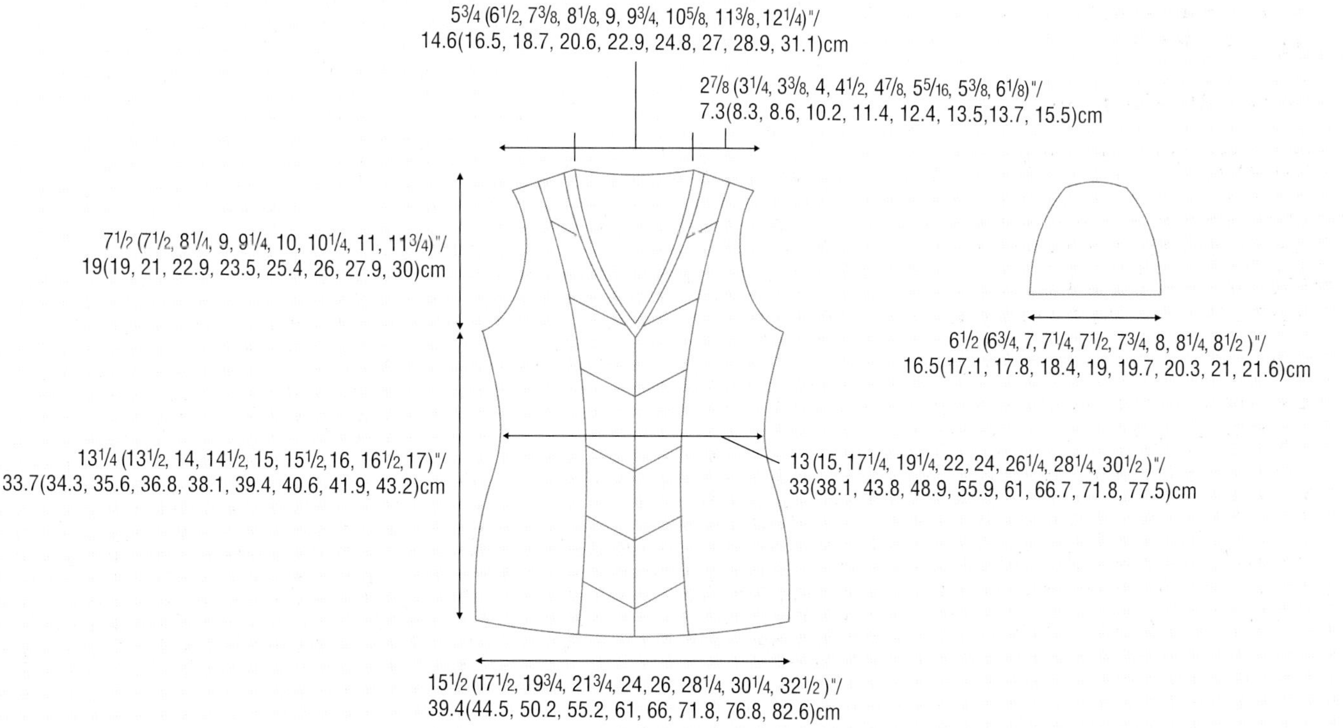
5 3/4 (6 1/2, 7 3/8, 8 1/8, 9, 9 3/4, 10 5/8, 11 3/8, 12 1/4)"/
14.6(16.5, 18.7, 20.6, 22.9, 24.8, 27, 28.9, 31.1)cm
2 7/8 (3 1/4, 3 3/8, 4, 4 1/2, 4 7/8, 5 5/16, 5 3/8, 6 1/8)"/
7.3(8.3, 8.6, 10.2, 11.4, 12.4, 13.5,13.7, 15.5)cm
7 1/2 (7 1/2, 8 1/4, 9, 9 1/4, 10, 10 1/4, 11, 11 3/4)"/
19(19, 21, 22.9, 23.5, 25.4, 26, 27.9, 30)cm
6 1/2 (6 3/4, 7, 7 1/4, 7 1/2, 7 3/4, 8, 8 1/4, 8 1/2)"/
16.5(17.1, 17.8, 18.4, 19, 19.7, 20.3, 21, 21.6)cm
13 1/4 (13 1/2, 14, 14 1/2, 15, 15 1/2,16, 16 1/2,17)"/
33.7(34.3, 35.6, 36.8, 38.1, 39.4, 40.6, 41.9, 43.2)cm
13 (15, 17 1/4, 19 1/4, 22, 24, 26 1/4, 28 1/4, 30 1/2)"/
33(38.1, 43.8, 48.9, 55.9, 61, 66.7, 71.8, 77.5)cm
15 1/2 (17 1/2, 19 3/4, 21 3/4, 24, 26, 28 1/4, 30 1/4, 32 1/2)"/
39.4(44.5, 50.2, 55.2, 61, 66, 71.8, 76.8, 82.6)cm

SHAPING

BO 6 (6, 6, 8, 8, 11, 11, 13, 13) sts at beg of next 2 rows.

Dec 1 st each side every other row on RS rows 8 (6, 7, 9, 13, 11, 20, 24, 30) times.

Dec 1 st each side every other RS row 9 (12, 13, 13, 12, 14, 11, 10, 8) times.

BO 4 (4, 4, 4, 5, 5, 5, 6, 6) sts at beg of next 4 rows.

BO rem 16 (18, 20, 22, 22, 24, 24, 24, 28) sts.

SEAMING

Seam shoulders together using 3-needle BO. Sew side seams together. Place rem back sts on waste yarn. Using 4.0 mm needles and Yarn B, k2tog across to end. Work even 6 rows in St st. Cut yarn, leaving a 30"/76 cm tail.

Fold over sts to wrong side of back, forming a facing, and then using yarn tail, invisibly sew open sts to back so edge is about 10 rows below neck opening, stretching folded hem slightly to prevent neck sts from rolling. To sew, do not pull yarn completely through work, but through a single purl bump on inside of back panel.

Sew sides of front center panel to inside edges of front outside panels, placing top edge of front center panel 2 (2¼, 2½, 2¾, 3, 3¼, 3½, 3¾, 4)"/ 5 (5.6, 6.4, 6.9, 7.6, 8.2, 8.9, 9.5, 10.2) cm from shoulder seam. Sew through pintucks to conceal the edges in the seam.

Sew sleeve seam, then sew sleeves into armholes.

WORK ATTACHED I-CORD

Using 3.5 mm dpns and Yarn B, CO 6 sts. Work attached I-cord as follows around neck edge.

Do not turn work, but slide sts to other end of needle.

K5, sl1 as if to knit, p/u 1 st from edge, ssk slipped st with picked up edge st. Rep around entire neck edge.

Fasten off.

On each sleeve, with Yarn B, work 6-St attached I-cord in first row of Yarn A at hem.

At garment hem, with Yarn B, work 8-st attached I-cord in first row of Yarn B at hem, continuing across first row of front center panel and through both layers of the first pintuck at the very center of the panel.

FINISHING

Weave in ends. Block, stretching front center panel to match back length.

MARY ELLEN CAMISOLE

LUCINDA SNYDER

This functional camisole will become a staple in your wardrobe. Layered under a blazer for the office or worn on its own for a hot date, Mary Ellen is stylish and fun. The textured lace pattern drapes beautifully in the linen-mohair blend, while stockinette provides coverage on top. The construction is seamless, and the gorgeous ribbon straps provide a customizable fit.

SKILL LEVEL

Easy

SIZES

XS (S, M, L, XL)
34 (36, 38, 40, 42)"/
86 (91, 97, 102, 107) cm
Shown in size XS

FINISHED MEASUREMENTS

Chest: 34 (36, 38, 40, 42)"/
86 (91, 97, 102, 107) cm
Length: 23"/58 cm

MATERIALS AND TOOLS

Yarn

500 (500, 750, 750, 750) yd/457 (457, 686, 686, 686) m of worsted weight yarn, 49% linen, 35% kid mohair, 16% nylon, in cream

Needles

4.0 mm (size 6 U.S.) circular, 32" long/81 cm
or size to obtain correct gauge

GAUGE

22 sts and 26 rows = 4"/10.2 cm in St st
18 sts and 22 rows = 4"/10.2 cm in Modified Purse Stitch

Always take time to check your gauge.

THIS PROJECT WAS KNIT WITH:

Louet Kidlin Pixie (49% Linen, 35% Kid Mohair, 16% Nylon; 250 yd/100 g): 2 (2, 3, 3, 3) skeins, Cream (30)

4

PATTERN STITCH

MODIFIED PURSE STITCH

Multiple of 2 plus 1 sts.

Rnd 1: P1 * yo, k2tog * rep to the end.

Rep every round.

INSTRUCTIONS

BODY

Using a long-tail cast on, CO 188 (198, 208, 216, 230) sts. Pm and join to work in the rnd, being careful not to twist stitches. Work even in Modified Purse Stitch until piece measures 12"/31 cm from CO. Change to St st and work even for 4"/10.2 cm.

Divide Front and Back

K94 (99, 104, 108, 115) sts, pm, k remaining 94 (99, 104, 108, 115) sts. Cont working in St st and dec 1 st before and after each m (dec 4 sts) every other round 3 (2, 2, 1, 1) times—176 (190, 200, 212, 226) sts rem.

Work even in St st until piece measures 23"/58 cm or desired length from CO.

BO all sts.

FINISHING

Using ¾"/9.5 mm-wide ribbon of contrasting or similar color, weave in and out of every other st on last row of Modified Purse Stitch. Tie on the side to tighten the cami to fit. For the shoulder straps, knot ribbon to upper edge of front and back, approximately 5"/13 cm from sides.

MARY ELLEN CAMISOLE SCHEMATIC

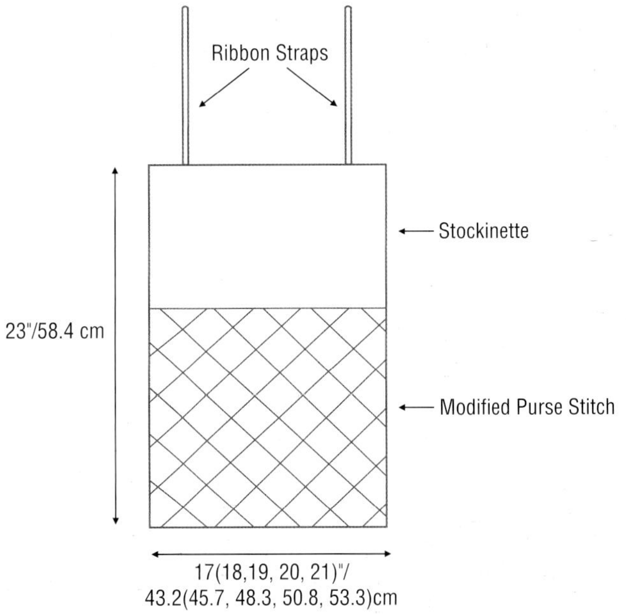
Ribbon Straps
Stockinette
23"/58.4 cm
Modified Purse Stitch
17(18,19, 20, 21)"/
43.2(45.7, 48.3, 50.8, 53.3)cm

CHAPTER 2

Cool Textures

PILATUS HAT AND SCARF SET

ERIKA SEELINGER

The snow-capped star topping this hat, along with the steep crags of the stitch pattern visible in the sheen of the yarns, reflects the alpine fantasy of Mt. Pilatus near Lake Lucerne, Switzerland. The lined band and density provided by its slipstitched body are terrific against even the most bitter winter winds. The herringbone and chevron patterns on both hat and scarf provide heaps of masculinity and are toned down just enough in a single color for your man to wear comfortably.

SKILL LEVEL

Easy/Intermediate

SIZES

Hat

Head circumference: 20"/51 cm

Scarf

Length: 65"/165 cm

MATERIALS AND TOOLS

Yarn

Yarn A: 550 yd/503 m (for set) of DK weight yarn, 50% merino wool, 50% silk, in ecru

Yarn B: 300 yd/274 m (for set) of worsted weight yarn, 100% merino wool, in natural

Needles

3.75 mm (size 5 U.S.) circular, 32"/81 cm long (optional)

4.25 mm (size 6 U.S.) circular, 32"/81 cm long

4.25 mm (size 6 U.S.) circular, 16"/41 cm long or dpns

5.5 mm (size 9 U.S.) circular, 32"/81 cm long

5.5 mm (size 9 U.S.) circular, 16"/41 cm long or dpns

or size to obtain correct gauge

Notions

Stitch markers

Crochet hook

GAUGE

24 sts = 4"/10.2 cm in St st on 4.25 mm needles

24 sts = 4"/10.2 cm in Zebra Chevron patt on 4.25 mm needles

24 sts = 4"/10.2 cm in Woven Herringbone patt on 5.5 mm needles

Always take time to check your gauge.

PATTERN STITCHES

WOVEN HERRINGBONE

Multiple of 4 sts +2.
Note: Written instructions shown below.

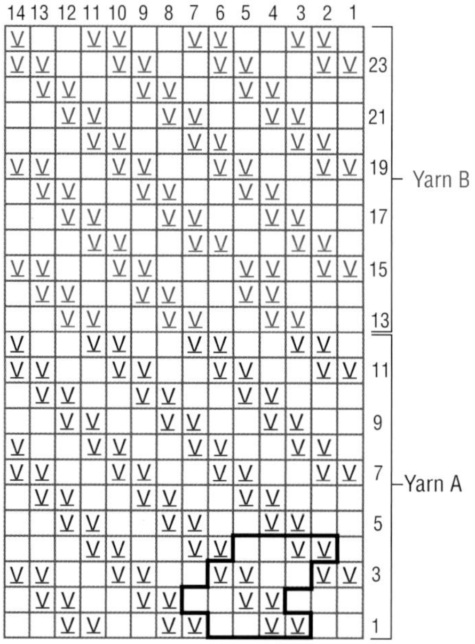
14 13 12 11 10 9 8 7 6 5 4 3 2 1
23
21
19
17
15
13
11
9
7
5
3
1
Yarn B
Yarn A

STITCH KEY

Highlighted repeat in round

RS: Knit stitch.
WS: Purl stitch.

Slip wyif
RS: Slip 1 stitch as if to purl, holding yarn in front.
WS: Slip 1 stitch as if to purl, holding yarn in back.

THIS PROJECT WAS KNIT WITH:

Louisa Harding Grace Wool & Silk (50% merino wool, 50% silk; 110 yd/50 g): 5 balls for set, Ecru (01)

3

Yarn B: Kraemer Yarns Janice (100% merino wool; 300 yd/100 g): 1 skein for set, Natural

4

PATTERN NOTES

When following the charts rather than line-by-line directions, be alert to how the patterns change in the round.

Remember to always read the chart from right to left when knitting in the round. For flat knitting, read knit rows right to left, and purl rows left to right.

Note that the Woven Herringbone pattern is knit in the round for the hat, but is knit flat for the scarf. Be aware that this changes where the yarn is held for purl row slipped stitches. In the round version of Woven Herring-bone, all slipped stitches are passed with yarn in front; in the flat knitting version, on purl rows the stitches are slipped with the yarn in back. The yarn will not be carried up the side due to the size of the stripes. If you prefer a longer scarf, simply add stitches in 4 sts increments. A longer scarf will require additional yarn.

The use of a crochet cast-on ensures that the edge will look exactly like the bind-off. Make a loop with yarn and put on left hand needle. With crochet hook, draw a loop through the first loop and hold under the needle. Draw yarn over needle and hook through the loop. (2 sts on needle) Repeat until 1 less number of required sts are on needle. Put remaining loop on hook.

Work your pattern as needed.

This pattern may challenge your standing ideas of what needle sizes to use when. The Woven Herringbone pattern is so dense that you will go up three U.S. needle sizes from those used to create the stockinette gauge, in order to get a proper drape for the scarf.

INSTRUCTIONS

PILATUS HAT

Using the long tail cast on and 4.25 mm 16"/41 cm-long circular needles, CO 120 sts with Yarn A. Join for knit-ting in the rnd, being careful not to twist, and pm to indicate the beg of the rnd. Work in St st for 2¾"/6.9 cm.

Next rnd: Kfb, k to 1 st before end of rnd, kfb—122 sts.

Purl 1 rnd for turning rnd.

Knit 2 rnds.

ZEBRA CHEVRON

Multiple of 24 sts.

Note: Written instructions shown below.

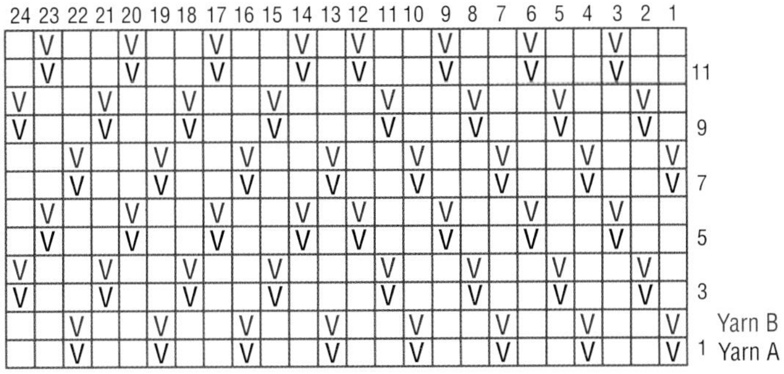
24 23 22 21 20 19 18 17 16 15 14 13 12 11 10 9 8 7 6 5 4 3 2 1
11
9
7
5
3
Yarn B
1 Yarn A

STITCH KEY

☐ **RS:** Knit stitch.

[V] Slip
RS: Slip 1 stitch as if to purl, holding yarn at back.

[V] Slip
WS: Slip 1 stitch as if to purl, holding yarn in front.

Change to 5.5 mm 16"/41 cm-long circular needles and begin Woven Herringbone patt.

Rnd 1: K2, *(sl2 wyif, k2); rep from *to end of rnd.

Rnd 2: K3, *(sl2 wyif, k2) to last 3 sts, end sl2 wyif, k1.

Rnd 3: Sl2 wyif *(k2, sl2 wyif); rep from * to end of rnd.

Rnd 4: K1 *(sl2 wyif, k2); repeat from * to last 5 sts, end sl2 wyif, k3.

Rnds 5–12: Rep rnds 1–4 twice more.

Break yarn.

Change to Yarn B.

Note: *Be sure to remember to shift the direction of the stitch pattern to the alternating 12 rows when changing colors.*

Rnd 13: Sl2 wyif *(k2, sl2 wyif); rep from * to end of rnd.

Rnd 14: K3, *(sl2 wyif, k2); rep from * to last 3 sts, end sl2 wyif, k1.

Rnd 15: K2, *(sl2 wyif, k2); rep from * to end of rnd.

Rnd 16: K1, *(sl2 wyif, k2); rep from * to last 5 sts, end sl 2 wyif, k3.

Rnds 17–24: Rep rnds 13–16 twice more. Break yarn.

Change to Yarn A and rep rnds 1–11.

Change to 4.25 mm needles and work rnd 12.

Weave in all ends to encase them in hat band.

Rnd 25: Fold hat band to inside on purl row, and k each st on needle together with 1 st from cast-on row, creating a double-layer hat band.

Rnd 26: P2tog, p to last 2 sts, p2tog—120 sts total.

Change to Yarn B and begin Zebra Chevron patt.

Note: *In the round, all slipped stitches are slipped with the yarn in back, opposite of the hat band's Herringbone pattern.*

Carry both yarns up the back of the hat by pulling the new working yarn over and around the previously used yarn every two rows. This will result in a neatly twisted line running up the inside back of the hat.

Rnds 1–2: With Yarn B, *(sl 1 wyib, k2); rep from * to end of rnd.

Rnds 3–4: Change to Yarn A. *[K1, sl1 wyib, (k2, sl1 wyib) 3 times, k3, (sl1 wyib, k2) 3 times, sl1 wyib]; rep from * to end of round (5 repeats total).

Rnds 5 6: With Yarn B, *[k2, (sl1 wyib, k2) 3 times, sl1, k1, sl1, (k2, sl1 wyib) 3 times, k1]; rep from * to end of round (5 repeats total).

Rnds 7–8: With Yarn A, *(sl 1 wyib, k2); rep from * to end of rnd.

Rnds 9–10: With Yarn B, *[k1, sl1 wyib, (k2, sl1 wyib) 3 times, k3, (sl1 wyib, k2) 3 times, sl1 wyib]; rep from * to end of round (5 repeats total).

Rnds 11–12: With Yarn A, *[k2, (sl1 wyib, k2) 3 times, sl1, k1, sl1, (k2, sl1 wyib) 3 times, k1]; rep from * to end of round (5 repeats total).

Rep rnds 1–12 for 5½" to 6"/14 to 15 cm, ending after completing row 6 in Yarn B. Break yarn.

Change to Yarn A and beg Dec Rnds.

Rnd 1: **K1, k2tog, k7, ssk.** Rep between ** 10 times to end of round—100 sts.

Rnd 2: K to end of round.

Rnd 3: **K1, k2tog, k5, ssk.** Rep between ** 10 times to end of round—80 sts.

Rnd 4: **K1, k2tog, k3, ssk.** Rep between ** to end of round—60 sts.

Rnd 5: **K1, k2tog, k1, ssk.* Rep between ** to end of round—40 sts

Rnd 6: **K1, k2tog, ssk.* Rep between ** to end of round—20 sts.

Break yarn, leaving a tail. Thread through tapestry needle and pull through remaining 20 sts. Tighten and fasten off. Weave in end securely.

PILATUS SCARF

Using a crochet CO on a 3.75 mm circular needle and Yarn A, CO 338 sts. Change to 4.25 mm circular needle, and work 2 rows of St st.

Change to 5.5 mm circular needle, and begin Woven Herringbone patt.

Row 1 (RS): K2, **sl2 kwise wyif, k2.** Rep between ** to end.

Row 2 (WS): P1, **sl2 pwise wyib, p2.**

Rep between ** to last 5 sts, sl2 pwise wyib, p3.

Row 3: Sl2 kwise wyif, **k2, sl2 kwise wyif.** Rep between ** to end.

Row 4: P3, **sl2 pwise wyib, p2.**

Rep between ** to last 3 sts, sl2 pwise wyib, p1.

Rows 5–12: Rep rows 1–4 two times more.

Row 13: Change to Yarn B. Sl2 wyif, **k2, sl2 wyif.** Rep between ** to end.

Row 14: P1, **sl2 wyib, p2.** Rep between ** to last 5 sts, sl2 wyib, p3.

Row 15: K2, **sl2 wyif, k2.** Rep between ** to end.

Row 16: P3, **sl2 wyib, p2.** Rep between ** to last 3 sts, sl2 wyib, p1.

Rows 17–24: Rep rows 13–16 two times more.

Repeat rows 1–24, breaking and changing yarn after completing row 12 and row 24, a total of three times—72 rows completed.

Change to Yarn A and work rows 1–11. Then, change to 4.25 mm needle and work row 12 only—84 rows total.

FINISHING

BO. Weave in ends.
Block to size.

SLIP-STITCH CORSET

CONNIE CHANG CHINCHIO

The lambswool, angora, and cashmere blend softens the structural slipped stitches used in this corsetlike strapless top. Closed with a row of delicate buttons set in a henley placket and with a thread of elastic woven through the ribbed border, this top can be worn alone or over a close-fitting blouse.

SKILL LEVEL
Intermediate

SIZES
XS (S, M, L, XL, 2X)
31 (33½, 37¼, 41, 44¾, 49¾)"/
79 (85, 95, 104, 114, 126) cm
Shown in size S

FINISHED MEASUREMENTS
Chest: 31 (34½, 37¼, 41, 44¾, 50)"/
70 (85, 95 104, 114, 127) cm
Length: 13½ (13½, 14, 15, 15½,
15½)"/34 (34, 36, 38, 39, 39) cm

MATERIALS AND TOOLS
Yarn
600 (600, 600, 1200, 1200, 1200) yd/
549 (549, 549, 1097, 1097, 1097) m
of DK weight yarn, 80% lambswool,
10% angora, 10% cashmere, in natural

Needles
3.75 mm (size 5 U.S.) circular or straight
3.5 mm (size 4 U.S.) circular, any
length, to work borders
or size to obtain correct gauge

Notions
Darning needles
Five small cream buttons
Elastic thread

GAUGE
25½ sts and 41 rows = 4"/10.2 cm
in Diagonal Slip Stitch
24 sts and 32 rows = 4"/10.2 cm
in St st

Always take time to check your gauge.

THIS PROJECT WAS KNIT WITH:
Yarntini (80% lambswool, 10% angora, 10% cashmere; 300 yd/100 g); 2 (2, 2, 4, 4, 4) skeins, Natural

3

PATTERN NOTES
Do not slip stitches fewer than 3 sts in from the edge.

PATTERN STITCHES
DIAGONAL SLIP STITCH
Multiple of 4 + 5 sts.

Row 1 (RS): K1, *sl1, k3; rep from * to end.

Row 2: *P3, sl1; rep from * to next to last st, p1.

Row 3: K1, *drop next slipped st off the left hand needle to front of work, k2, p/u dropped st and k it, k1; rep from * to next to last st, k1.

Row 4: P.

Row 5: K3, *k2, sl1, k1; rep from * to last 2 sts, k2.

Row 6: P2, *p1, sl1, p2; rep from * to last 3 sts, p3.

Row 7: K3, *sl next 2 sts, drop next slipped st off left hand needle to front of work, put 2 slipped sts from right hand needle to left hand needle, p/u dropped slipped st and k it, k3; rep from * to last 2 sts, k2.

Row 8: P.

INSTRUCTIONS
BACK
With 3.5 mm needles, CO 93 (101, 111, 122, 133, 148) sts.

Work 9 rows k1, p1 rib, ending with a RS row. Change to 3.75 mm needles. Inc Row (WS): P across, inc 8 (8, 10, 11, 12, 13) sts evenly across row—101 (109, 121, 133, 145, 161) sts rem.

Work in Diagonal Slip Stitch patt until piece measures 2 (2, 2, 2½, 2½, 2½)"/ 5 (5, 5, 6.4, 6.4, 6.4) cm from beg of piece, ending with a WS row.

Waist Shaping
Cont to work in Slip Stitch patt, shape waist as follows.

Dec Row: Work 2 sts, ssk, work to 2 sts before end, k2tog, work 2 sts.

Work this dec row every 8 rows 3 times more—8 sts dec, 93 (101, 113, 125, 137, 153) sts rem.

Work even for 2"/5 cm, ending with a WS row.

Bust Shaping
Inc Row: Work 2 sts, m1l, work to 2 sts before end, m1r, work 2 sts.

Work this inc row every 14 rows 3 times more—8 sts inc, 101 (109, 121, 133, 145, 161) sts rem.

Work even until piece measures 12¼ (12¼, 12¾, 13¾, 14¼, 14¼)"/31 (31, 32, 35, 36, 36) cm, ending on a WS row.

Change to 3.5 mm needles.

Work k1, p1 rib. AT THE SAME TIME dec 8 (8, 10, 11, 12, 13) sts evenly across row—93 (101, 111, 122, 133, 148) sts rem.

Work in k1, p1 rib for 9 rows more. BO 93 (101, 111, 122, 133, 148) sts.

Piece should measure 13½ (13½, 14, 15, 15½, 15½)"/34 (34, 36, 38, 39, 39)cm.

FRONT

Work as for back until after second bust increase—97 (105, 117, 129, 141, 157) sts rem.

Work even for 3 rows, ending on a WS row.

Split for Neck Opening

Work 47 (51, 57, 63, 69, 77) sts, BO 4 sts, work 46 (50, 56, 62, 68, 76) sts.

Attach another yarn to placket opening edge of the left front and, working both sides at the same time, cont working as for back until piece measures same length as back before beg k1, p1 rib.

Change to 3.5 mm needles and work both sides in k1, p1 rib. AT THE SAME TIME dec 4 (4, 5, 6, 6, 7) sts evenly spaced across row on left front and 4 (4, 5, 5, 6, 6) sts evenly spaced across row on right front—43 (47, 52, 57, 63, 70) sts rem on the left front and 42 (46, 51, 57, 62, 70) sts rem on the right front.

BO all sts.

FINISHING

Block pieces to measurements.
Sew side seams using mattress st.

Buttonhole Band (Left Front)

With RS facing up, starting at the top left front, p/u 34 (34, 37, 41, 44, 44) sts along placket opening edge.

Work in k1, p1 rib for 7 rows.

BO in k1, p1 rib.

Buttonhole Band (Right Front)

With RS facing, starting at the bottom of the placket opening, p/u 34 (34, 37, 41, 44, 44) sts along placket opening edge.

Work in k1, p1 rib for 3 rows, ending on a WS row.

Buttonhole Row: K5 (5, 4, 4, 6, 6), *BO 2 sts for buttonhole, k4 (4, 5, 6, 6, 6); rep from * to last 3 (3, 3, 3, 4, 4) sts, k3 (3, 3, 3, 4, 4).

On next row, work in k1, p1 rib, CO 2 sts over each 2 st BO. Work in k1, p1 rib for 2 more rows.

BO in k1, p1 rib.

Sew buttons to button band, spacing them to match buttonholes.

Sew the bottom of the button and buttonhole bands to the bottom of the placket opening.

Block again if desired.

Thread a piece of elastic cord measuring slightly less than the width of the corset through the top of the corset. Weave in ends.

SLIP-STITCH CORSET SCHEMATIC

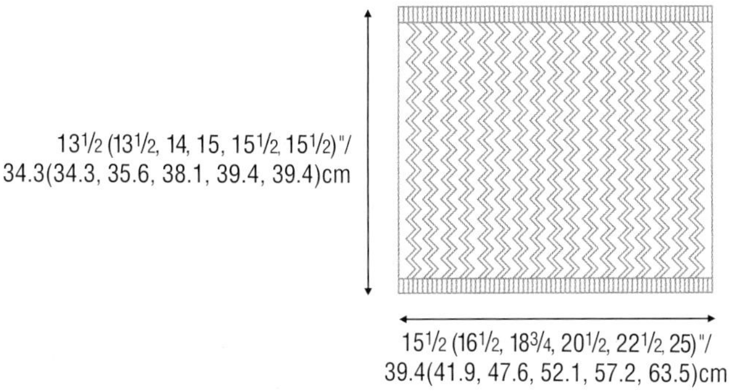
13½ (13½, 14, 15, 15½, 15½)"/
34.3(34.3, 35.6, 38.1, 39.4, 39.4)cm
15½ (16½, 18¾, 20½, 22½, 25)"/
39.4(41.9, 47.6, 52.1, 57.2, 63.5)cm

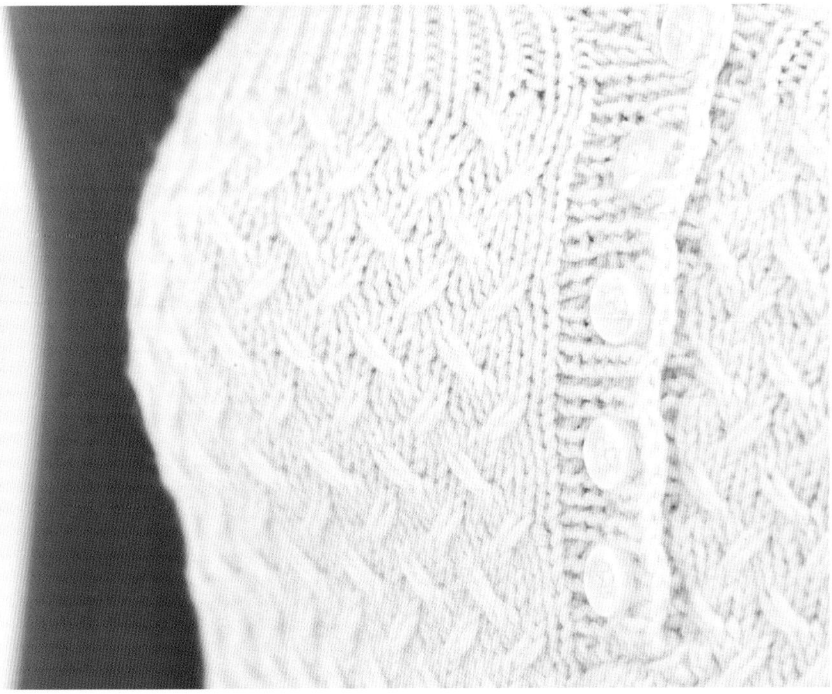

BUBBLE BATH BABY DOLL

KATE SONNICK

The softness of this romantic baby doll top feels like you just slipped into a tub full of bubbles. Floaty and sheer, it's an easy, flirty layer over a slip dress. Or dress it down over a tiny tee and pair it with your favorite skinny jeans or leggings. The sleeveless, tunic-length top is knit in stockinette with a deep-V neckline, smocked waist, and gently ruffled sleeve detail. It's knit in luscious silk mohair and silk on large needles to achieve a transparent, lightweight, and softly draping fabric.

SKILL LEVEL

Intermediate

SIZES

S (M, L, XL)
34 (38, 42, 46)"/86 (97, 107, 117) cm
Shown in size S

FINISHED MEASUREMENTS

Bust: 34 (38, 42, 46)"/
86 (97, 106, 117) cm
Length: 26½ (27½, 28, 29)"/
67 (70, 71, 74) cm

MATERIALS AND TOOLS

Yarn

687 (916, 916, 1145) yd/
628 (838, 838 1047) m of light worsted weight yarn, 70% super kid mohair, 30% silk, in cream

Needles

5.5 mm (size 9 U.S.) straight
or size to obtain correct gauge
Lace-style extra-pointy needles are recommended.

Notions

Tapestry needle
Stitch markers
Stitch holder

GAUGE

18 sts and 24 rows = 4"/
10.2 cm in St st

Always take time to check your gauge.

THIS PROJECT WAS KNIT WITH:

Rowan "Kidsilk Haze" (70% super kid mohair, 30% silk; 229 yd/25 g): 3 (4, 4, 5) balls, Cream (634)

PATTERN NOTES

This pullover is worked in two pieces, with the smocked band only on the front. Before smocking, the front width is larger than back width. Smocked band is worked in 3x1 Rib that is later smocked according to the smocking technique shown on page 136.

The back is worked in St st.
The ruffle is worked by picking up stitches along the top sleeve edge. Due to the fine yarn and large needle size used, extra-pointy (lace-style) knitting needles are recommended.

PATTERN STITCH

3X1 RIB

Row 1 (RS): *P3, k1; rep from * to end.

Row 2: P the purl sts and k the knit sts.

Rep row 2.

INSTRUCTIONS

FRONT

Using 5.5 mm needles, CO 136 (152, 176, 192) sts.

Work in St st for 12 (13, 13, 13½)"/30 (33, 33, 34) cm, ending with WS row.

Shape Waist

Row 1: P3, k1, rep to end of row, ending with k1.

Row 2: K the k sts and p the p sts. Work even in 3x1 Rib for 14 rows, ending with WS row.

Next row: P3, k4, *k5tog, p3. Rep from * to last 9 sts: k5, p3, k1—76 (84, 96, 104) sts.

Work even in St st until piece measures 4 (4, 3½, 3½)"/10 (10, 9, 9) cm above ribbing, ending with a WS row.

Shape Neck

Each side of neck is worked separately.

K38 (42, 48, 52) sts, turn, placing rem sts on a holder. Cont to work in St st, dec 1 st every other row at neck edge 5 (5, 6, 6) times, then every 4 (4, 5, 5) rows 10 times. AT THE SAME TIME, when piece measures 19½ (20½, 20½, 21½)"/50 (52, 52, 55) cm from CO edge, beg armhole shaping.

Shape Armholes

BO 4 (5, 6, 7) sts at side for armhole.

Dec 1 st at armhole edge on next 9 (11, 15, 16) rows.

Work even until armhole measures 7 (7, 7½, 7½)"/17.8 (17.8, 19, 19) cm, ending with WS row—10 (11, 11, 13) sts.

Shape Shoulders

Bind off 5 (5, 5, 6) sts at beg of next 2 RS rows.

Bind off rem 0 (1, 1, 1) sts.
Move sts on holder to needle and attach yarn. With RS facing, work as for other side, reversing shaping.

BACK

With 5.5 mm needles, CO 90 (94, 100, 104) sts.

Work in St st for 10 (10, 20, 20) rows, ending with WS row.

Dec 1 (0, 0, 0) st each side.

Then, dec 1 st each side every 15 (15, 30, 30) rows 6 (5, 2, 0) times—76 (84, 96, 104) sts.

Work even in St st until back measures same as front to armhole.

Work armhole shaping on both sides as for front.

When armhole measures 7 (7, 7½, 7½)"/17.8 (17.8, 19, 19) cm, begin neck and shoulder shaping, ending with a WS row.

Shape Shoulders and Neck

Next row: K10 (11, 11, 13) sts.

Turn, placing rem 40 (41, 43, 45) sts on a holder.

Work each side of neck separately as follows.

Work 1 row even.

Next row, BO 5 (5, 5, 6) sts at shoulder edge; work to end.

Work 1 row even.

Next row, BO rem sts—5 (6, 6, 7) sts.

Move sts on holder to needle and attach yarn.

With RS facing, BO center 30 (30, 32, 32) sts; work to end.

Work as for other side, reversing shapings.

FINISHING

Lightly seam edges; do not press ribbing at waistband. Join shoulder seams.

RUFFLE SLEEVE DETAIL

On armhole edge, with RS facing, p/u and k20 sts so there are 10 sts on each side of shoulder seam.

Row 2 and all even number rows: P.

Row 3: Kfb of every stitch—40 sts.

Row 5: Repeat row 3—80 sts.

Row 7: Rep row 3—160 sts.

Row 8: P.

Bind off. Sew ends of ruffle to armhole edge.

Repeat for other side.

SMOCKED WAIST BAND

See page 136 for complete smocking instructions.

FINISHING

Sew side seams. Press seams lightly.

BUBBLE BATH BABY DOLL SCHEMATIC

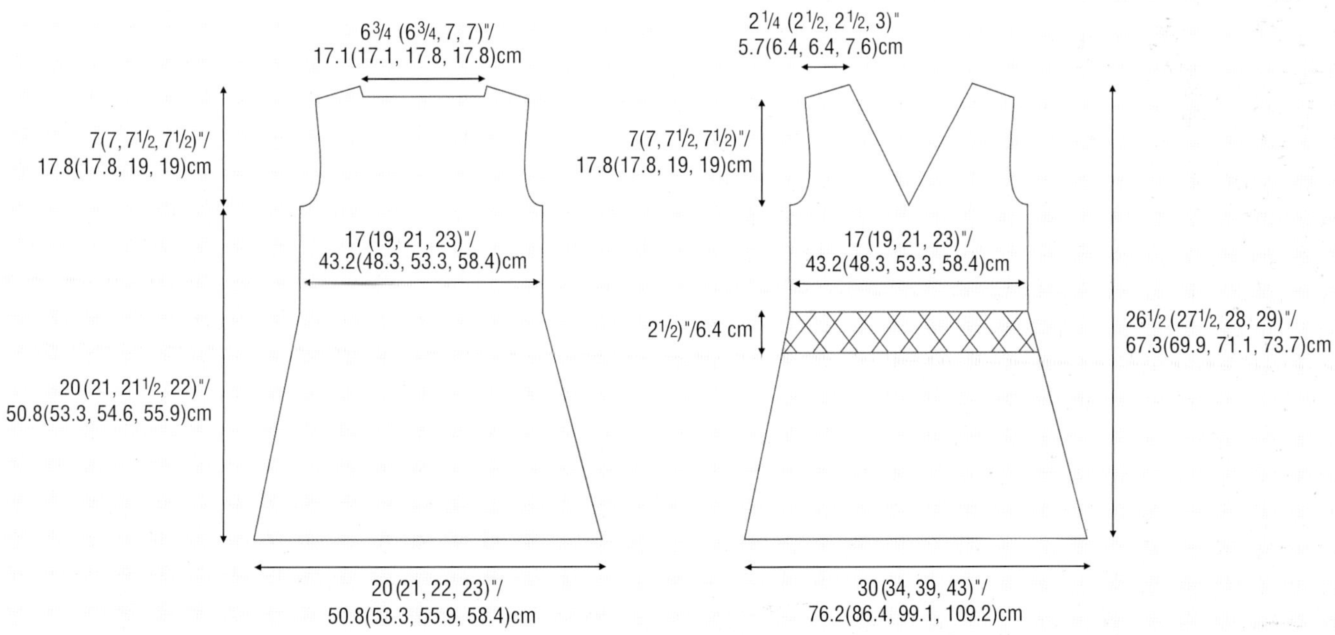
6¾ (6¾, 7, 7)"/
17.1(17.1, 17.8, 17.8)cm
7(7, 7½, 7½)"/
17.8(17.8, 19, 19)cm
17 (19, 21, 23)"/
43.2(48.3, 53.3, 58.4)cm
20(21, 21½, 22)"/
50.8(53.3, 54.6, 55.9)cm
20 (21, 22, 23)"/
50.8(53.3, 55.9, 58.4)cm
2¼ (2½, 2½, 3)"
5.7(6.4, 6.4, 7.6)cm
7(7, 7½, 7½)"/
17.8(17.8, 19, 19)cm
17 (19, 21, 23)"/
43.2(48.3, 53.3, 58.4)cm
2½)"/6.4 cm
26½ (27½, 28, 29)"/
67.3(69.9, 71.1, 73.7)cm
30 (34, 39, 43)"/
76.2(86.4, 99.1, 109.2)cm

CROSSHATCH TOP

ZOË VALETTE

This luxurious blouse will lift your spirits and flatter your body. Knit in stunning noble fibers, the Crosshatch Top will awaken every sense. The stitch patterns create subtle shaping, while the elegant V-neck shows just enough skin.

THIS PROJECT WAS KNIT WITH:

Sublime Cashmere Merino Silk DK, (75% merino, 20% silk, 5% cashmere, 127 yd/50 g): 6 (7, 8, 9, 10, 11) skeins, Natural (0003)

PATTERN NOTES

This top also looks adorable when made without sleeves. If you make it sleeveless, simply slip the first stitch of every row in the armholes to make a neater edge.

PATTERN STITCH

Seed Stitch

Rnd 1: *K1, p1, rep from *.

Rnd 2: *P1, k1, rep from *.

INSTRUCTIONS

BACK

Using invisible or provisional cast on and waste yarn, CO 94 (104, 116, 126, 138, 148) sts. Work 11 rows in St st, ending with a WS row. Remove waste yarn and place all provisional CO stitches on spare needle. With the active needle in front and wrong sides together, ktog one st on front needle with one st on back needle, creating a tubular hem.

Cont working even in St st until piece measures 3"/7.6 cm from hem edge.

Pm 24 (25, 25, 24, 24, 24) sts in from either edge to indicate where decs will be made.

Work decs on the next and every 10 rows 6 times as follows: K to first marker, sm, ssk, k to 2 sts before next marker, k2tog, sm, k to end of row—82 (92, 104, 114, 126, 136) sts rem.

Work even in St st until piece measures 11"/28 cm from hem edge, ending with a WS row.

Next RS row for your size:

XS: K to 1st marker, sm, sl2, k1, psso, *k4, ssk, k2tog, rep from * 3 times, end k4, sl2, k1, psso, k1, sm, k to end.

S: K to 1st marker, sm, k1, ssk, *k4, ssk, k2tog, rep from * 4 times, end k4, k2tog, k1, sm, k to end.

M: K to 1st marker, sm, k1, ssk, (k4, ssk) twice, (k4, ssk, k2tog) twice, (k4, k2tog) 3 times, k1, sm, k to end.

L: K to 1st marker, sm, k1, ssk, (k4, ssk) 4 times, (k4, k2tog) 5 times, k1, sm, k to end.

XL: K to 1st marker, sm, k1, ssk, (k4, ssk) twice, k4, (k4, ssk) twice, (k4, k2tog) twice, k4, (k4, k2tog) 3 times, k1, sm, k to end.

2X: K to 1st marker, sm, k1, ssk, *k4, (k4, ssk) twice, rep from * once more; (k4, k2tog) twice, k4, (k4, k2tog) twice, k8, k2tog, k1, sm, k to end.

24 (32, 44, 56, 68, 78) sts rem between markers.

SKILL LEVEL

Intermediate

SIZES

XS (S, M, L, XL, 2X)
28 (32, 36, 40, 44, 48)"/
71 (81, 91, 102, 112, 122) cm
Shown in size S

FINISHED MEASUREMENTS

Chest: 30 (34, 38, 42, 46, 50)"/
76 (86, 97, 107, 117, 127) cm
Length: 26"/66 cm

MATERIALS AND TOOLS

Yarn

762 (889, 1016, 1143, 1270, 1397) yd/
697 (813, 929, 1045, 1161, 1277) m
of DK weight yarn, 75% merino,
20% silk, 5% cashmere, in natural

Needles

4.0 mm (size 6 U.S.) straight
or size to obtain gauge

Notions

Crochet hook and waste yarn in similar gauge for provisional cast on
Stitch markers
Tapestry needles

GAUGE

22 sts and 28 rows =
4"/10.2 cm in St st
20 sts and 36 rows =
4"/10.2 cm in Seed st

Always take time to check your gauge.

Back Bodice

Rows 1–4: Beg on WS, work 4 rows even in Reverse St st (k on WS, p on RS).

Rows 5–8: Work 4 rows in St st.

Row 9: Work 1 row Reverse St st and kfb in first and last st.

Rows 10–12: Work 3 rows Reverse St st.

Repeat rows 5–12 six more times.

Work 2 rows even in St st.
86 (96, 108, 118, 130, 140) sts.

Armhole Shaping

BO 3 (4, 5, 6, 7, 8) sts at beg of next 2 rows.

BO 2 (3, 4, 5, 6, 7) sts at beg of next 2 rows.

Work dec on next and every other RS row 2 (3, 3, 4, 4, 5) times as follows: K2, ssk, k to last 4 sts, k2tog, k2.

Note: *If you are making the sleeveless version, be sure to sl the 1st st on all rows.*

Work even until armhole measures 6 (6½, 7, 7½, 8, 8½)"/15.2 (16.5, 17.8, 19, 20.3, 21.6) cm, ending on a WS row.

Neck and Shoulder Shaping

K13 (14, 15, 16, 17, 18) sts, BO 46 (48, 52, 56, 62, 64) sts, k rem 13 (14, 15, 16, 17, 18) sts.

P back across left shoulder, attach new yarn to right shoulder, and begin short row shaping.

Row 1: P to last 5 (5, 5, 6, 6, 6) sts, w/t.

Row 2: Work even.

Row 3 (WS): Work to last 9 (10, 10, 11 12, 12) sts, w/t.

Row 4: Work even.

Row 5 (WS): P across, purling into wraps.

Place rem sts on holder.
Shape left shoulder as for right shoulder, reversing shaping. Place rem sts on holder.

FRONT

Work same as back to bodice piece measuring 11"/28 cm. 24 (32, 44, 56, 68, 78) sts rem btwn markers.

Front Bodice

Row 1 (WS): K to 1st marker, sm, p1, *yo, p5, yo, p1, rep from * 4 (5, 7, 9, 11, 13) times, p1, sm, k to end.

Row 2 (RS): P to 1st marker, sm, k1, *sl1, drop yo off the needle, k4, sl1, drop yo, rep from * 4 (5, 7, 9, 11, 13) times, k1, sm, p to end.

Row 3 (WS): K to 1st marker, sm, p1, *sl1, p4, sl1, rep from * 4 (5, 7, 9, 11, 13) times, p1, sm, k to end.

Row 4 (RS): P to 1st marker, sm, k1, *drop next st to front of work, k2, pick up dropped st and knit it, sl2, drop next st to front of work, sl same 2 sts back to left-hand needle, pick up dropped st and knit it, k2; rep from * 4 (5, 7, 9, 11, 13) times, k1, sm, p to end.

Note: *Be careful not to twist the dropped sts when replacing them on the needle.*

Row 5 (WS): P to 1st marker, sm, p1, *p2, (yo, p1) twice, p2; rep from * 4 (5, 7, 9, 11, 13) times, p1, sm, p to end.

Row 6 (RS): K to 1st marker, sm, k1, *k2, (sl1, drop yo) twice, k2, rep from * 4 (5, 7, 9, 11, 13) times, k1, sm, k to end.

Row 7 (WS): P to 1st marker, sm, p1, *p2, sl2, p2, rep from * 4 (5, 7, 9, 11, 13) times, p1, sm, p to end.

Row 8 (RS): K to 1st marker, sm, k1, * sl2, drop next st to front of work, sl same 2 sts back to left-hand needle, pick up dropped st and knit it, k2, drop next st to front of work, k2, pick up dropped st and knit it; rep from * 4 (5, 7, 9, 11, 13) times, p1, sm, p to end.
Rep these 8 rows 6 more times, and AT THE SAME TIME kfb into the 1st and last st of each Row 5.

Work 4 rows Reverse St st.

Work 3 rows of St st, placing a marker at the exact center of the front and ending with a WS row.

Neck and Armhole Shaping

Armhole and V-neck shaping are done at the same time.

Row 1 (RS): BO 3 (4, 5, 6, 7, 8) sts, k across left shoulder to center marker (beg of V-neck), attach new yarn for right shoulder, ssk, k to end of row. Cont working each side separately.

Right Side:

Row 2 (WS): BO 3 (4, 5, 6, 7, 8) sts for armhole, p to end.

Row 3: P2tog at neck edge, p to end.

Row 4 (RS): BO 2 (3, 4, 5, 6, 7) sts, k across.

Dec 1 at side edge every other RS row 2 (3, 3, 4, 4, 5) times.

AT THE SAME TIME dec 1 at neck edge every other row—k2, ssk, k to end—until 13 (14, 15, 16, 17, 18) sts rem.

Then work even in St st until armhole measures 6 (6½, 7, 7½, 8, 8½)"/15.2 (15.5, 16.5, 17.8, 19, 20.3, 21.6) cm. Complete short row shoulder shaping as for back. Place rem sts on holder. Repeat armhole and shoulder shaping for left side, reversing shaping. Place rem sts on holder.

SLEEVES (Make 2)

CO 59 (63, 67, 75, 81, 87) sts. Work 4 rows even in Seed st. Cont working in Seed st and at same time, BO 3 (4, 5, 6, 7, 8) at beginning of next 2 rows.

BO 2 (3, 4, 5, 6, 7) at beginning of next 2 rows.

BO 1 (2, 3, 4, 5, 6) at beginning of next 2 rows.

Work 2 rows even.

Dec 1 st at each side of next and every 4th row, 5 times.

Dec 1 st at each side of next and every other row, 3 times.

BO 5 (6, 7, 8, 9, 10) sts at the beg of next 2 rows.

BO rem sts.

FINISHING

Join shoulder seams together with a 3-needle BO. Sew sleeves in armhole. Sew side and sleeve seams in continuous seam.

CROSSHATCH TOP SCHEMATIC

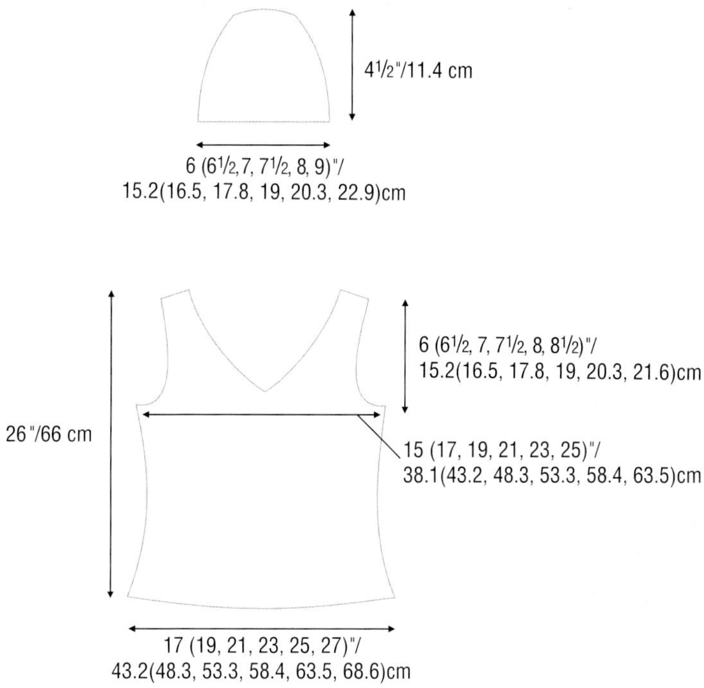
4½"/11.4 cm
6 (6½, 7, 7½, 8, 9)"/
15.2(16.5, 17.8, 19, 20.3, 22.9)cm
26"/66 cm
6 (6½, 7, 7½, 8, 8½)"/
15.2(16.5, 17.8, 19, 20.3, 21.6)cm
15 (17, 19, 21, 23, 25)"/
38.1(43.2, 48.3, 53.3, 58.4, 63.5)cm
17 (19, 21, 23, 25, 27)"/
43.2(48.3, 53.3, 58.4, 63.5, 68.6)cm

HUGO'S SWEATER

YAHAIRA FERREIRA

As one of my close friends gets ready for her first baby, I wanted to knit her something that would keep Hugo (our nickname for the baby) toasty, while also giving a nod to her famous raglan designs. Small repeat textures blend together to create a cozy sweater to curl up in on a chilly day. The unique yarn provides subtle shifts in texture, adding interest even through the stockinette portions. The resulting fabric is soft, light, warm, and luxurious to wear.

THIS PROJECT WAS KNIT WITH:

Pear Tree 12-ply Merino (100% merino wool; 170 yd/100 g): 2 (3, 3), natural

4

PATTERN NOTES

When working the Seed stitch yoke, be sure to decrease in pattern.

PATTERN STITCH

Seed Stitch

Rnd 1: *K1, p1, rep from *.

Rnd 2: *P1, k1, rep from *.

Garter Stitch (in the round)

Rnd 1: Knit

Rnd 2: Purl

INSTRUCTIONS

BODY

Hem

With 5.5 mm needles, CO 96 (102, 111) sts, pm and join for working in the rnd, taking care not to twist sts.

Work in k1, p2 rib for 48 (51, 55) sts, pm for side seam, work to end.

Work in k1, p1 rib for 1½ (1½, 2)"/3.8 (3.8, 5) cm.

Change to 6.0 mm circular needle and St st.

Size 2–4T

Inc 2 sts evenly across rnd.

Size 4–6

Dec 1 st at side seam.

All Sizes

Work even until piece measures 6 (7, 8)"/15.2 (17.8, 20.3) cm from CO edge.

Change to Seed st and work until piece measures 8 (9, 10)"/20.3 (22.9, 25.4) cm from CO edge.

Divide for Yoke

Work 2 (2, 3) sts, place the last 4 (4, 6) sts worked on a st holder, work to 2 (2, 3) sts beyond next marker, place the last 4 (4, 6) sts worked on st holder, work to end—44 (48, 50) sts for each front and back. Set aside and do not break yarn.

SKILL LEVEL

Intermediate

SIZES

6–18 months (2–4T, 4–6T)
Shown in size 2–4T

FINISHED MEASUREMENTS

Chest: 24 (26, 28)"/61 (66, 71) cm
Length: 13½ (15, 17)"/34 (38, 43) cm
Sleeve length: 8½ (10½, 12)"/22 (27, 31) cm

MATERIALS AND TOOLS

Yarn

340 (510, 510) yd/331 (466, 466) m of worsted weight yarn, 100% merino wool, in natural

Needles

6.0 mm (size 10 U.S.) circular, 24"/61 cm or 32"/81 cm long
5.5 mm (size 9 U.S.) circular, 24"/61 cm or 32"/81 cm long
6.0 mm (size 10 U.S.) dpns
5.5 mm (size 9 U.S.) dpns
or size to obtain gauge

Notions

Stitch markers
Stitch holder
Tapestry needle

GAUGE

16 sts and 22 rows = 4"/10.2 cm in St st with 6.0 mm needles

Always take time to check your gauge.

SLEEVES (Make 2)

With 5.5 mm dpns, CO 24 (24, 26) sts. Join for working in the rnd, and pm to indicate beg of rnd. Work in k1, p1 rib for 1½"/3.8 cm.

Change to 6.0 mm dpns and St st. Inc 2 (4, 3) sts evenly across next rnd—26 (28, 29) sts.

Inc Rnd: K1, m1l, k to last 2 sts, m1r, k1.

Work inc rnd every 9 (10, 11) rnds 1 (4, 3) times, then every 10 (0, 12) rnds 1 (0, 1) times—32 (36, 37) sts.

Change to garter st and work even until sleeve measures 8½ (10½, 12)"/ 22 (27, 31) cm from CO edge, ending on a p rnd.

Next rnd, k2 (2, 3), place the last 4 (4, 6) sts worked on a st holder, work to end—28 (32, 31) sts rem. Break yarn.

Work the sleeve sts onto the same circular needle, holding body next to the front 44 (48, 50) sts, pm, then work the back 44 (48, 50) sts. Set aside.

Work the second sleeve as the first.

Yoke

Note: *Maintain front/back in seed st and sleeves in garter stitch.*

Work 28 (32, 31) sts of left sleeve onto circular needle, holding body and right sleeve next to back sts, pm, work 44 (48, 50) sts for front—144 (160, 162) sts. Pm to indicate beg of new rnd (right sleeve raglan line).

Note: *Use different color markers for sleeve seams and front/back seams.*

Work 2 (2, 2) rounds even.

Dec Rnd: *K1, ssk, k to within 3 sts of next marker, k2tog, k1, sm, dec 1 st in patt, work in Seed st to within 2 sts of next marker, dec 1 st in patt, rep from * 1 more time—8 sts dec.

Rep front/back decreases on every 4 (4, 4) rnds 2 (2, 2) times more and then every 3 (3, 3) rnds 6 (7, 8) times.

AT THE SAME TME, rep sleeve decreases every 3 (3, 3) rnds 4 (3, 8) times more and every 2 (2, 2) rnds 7 (9, 4) times.

Begin working front and back sts in k1, p1 rib and AT THE SAME TIME cont sleeve dec 1 (2, 1) times—56 (60, 62) sts rem.

Collar

Change to 5.5mm dpns. Work 2 (2½, 3)"/5 (6.4, 7.6) cm in k1, p1 rib. BO using tubular BO.

FINISHING

Graft the sleeve and body sts together at the underarms. Block to size. Weave in all ends.

HUGO'S SWEATER SCHEMATIC

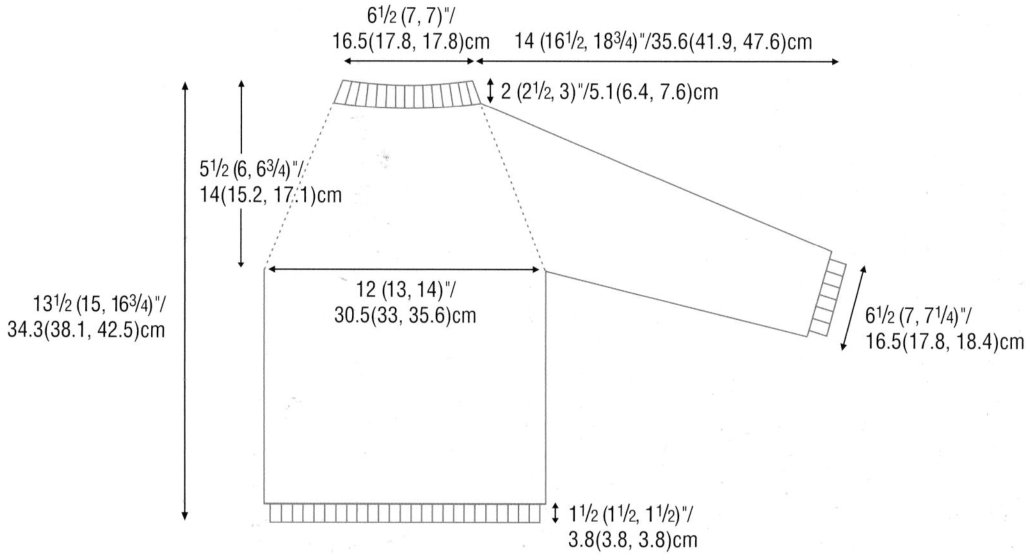
6½ (7, 7)"/
16.5(17.8, 17.8)cm
14 (16½, 18¾)"/35.6(41.9, 47.6)cm
2 (2½, 3)"/5.1(6.4, 7.6)cm
5½ (6, 6¾)"/
14(15.2, 17.1)cm
13½ (15, 16¾)"/
34.3(38.1, 42.5)cm
12 (13, 14)"/
30.5(33, 35.6)cm
6½ (7, 7¼)"/
16.5(17.8, 18.4)cm
1½ (1½, 1½)"/
3.8(3.8, 3.8)cm

ICE QUEEN

STEPHANIE PULFORD

Ice Queen is a versatile knit for many occasions. This elegant, form-fitting cardigan features a slimming diagonal motif with an unexpected sleeve cutout. The vertical lines of ribbing paired with a sharp V-neck will elongate your torso and attract your Prince Charming.

SKILL LEVEL
Experienced

SIZES
S (M, L)
32 (36, 40)"/81 (91, 102) cm
Shown in size S

FINISHED MEASUREMENTS
Chest: 32 (36, 40)"/81 (91, 102) cm
Length: 20¼ (22¾, 24¼)"/ 51.4 (52.7, 61.6) cm

MATERIALS AND TOOLS

Yarn
710 (994, 1278) yd/646 (909, 1169) m of sport weight yarn, 40% alpaca, 40% merino, 20% silk, in ecru

Needles
3.5 mm (size 4 U.S.) circular, 30"/76 cm long
3.5 mm (size 4 U.S.) dpns
or size to obtain gauge

Notions
Tapesty needle
Stitch holders

GAUGE
20 sts and 32 rows = 4"/10.2 cm in Diagonal patt

Always take time to check your gauge.

THIS PROJECT WAS KNIT WITH:
Jo Sharp Alpaca Silk Georgette (40% alpaca, 40% merino, 20% silk; 142 yd/50 g): 5 (7, 9) skeins, Ecru (752)

2

PATTERN STITCHES

Seed Rib (in the round)

Rnd 1: *K1, p2, k1, p1, repeat from * to end of rnd.

Rnd 2: *K1, p2, k2, repeat from * to end of rnd.

LEFT-LEANING DIAGONAL

Row 1: *K4, p1, repeat from * to end.

Row 2 and all even rows: If working in the round, k all sts. If not, p all sts.

Row 3: *P1, k4, repeat from * to end.

Row 5: *K1, p1, k3, repeat from * to end.

Row 7: *K2, p1, k2, repeat from * to end.

Row 9: *K3, p1, k1, repeat from * to end.

RIGHT-LEANING DIAGONAL

Row 1: *P1, k4, repeat from * to end.

Row 2 and all even rows: If working in the round, k all sts. If not, p all sts.

Row 3: *K4, p1, repeat from * to end.

Row 5: *K3, p1, k1, repeat from * to end.

Row 7: *K2, p1, k2, repeat from * to end.

Row 9: *K1, p1, k3, repeat from * to end.

INSTRUCTIONS

BODY

With circular needle, CO 161 (181, 201), pm (beg of rnd and center front rib), and join to work in the rnd.

Rnd 1: P2, k4, (p2, k2) 2 times, p2, k4, p2, pm (end center front rib), work in Seed Rib to end of rnd, sm.

Rnd 2–7: Rep rnd 1.

Rnd 8: P2, k4, (p2, k2) 2 times, p2, k4, p2, sm, k4, *p1, k4, rep from * to end of rnd, sm.

Rnd 9: P2, k4, (p2, k2) 2 times, p2, k4, p2, sm, k to end of rnd, sm.

Rep rnds 8 and 9 until work measures 10 (12, 13)"/25 (31, 33) cm.

Next rnd: Rep rnd 8.

Next rnd: P2, k4, (p2, k2) 2 times, p2, k4, p2, sm, k30 (35, 40), pm, k40 (45, 50), pm, k40 (45, 50), pm, k29 (34, 39) to end of rnd, sm.

Right-Leaning Diagonal

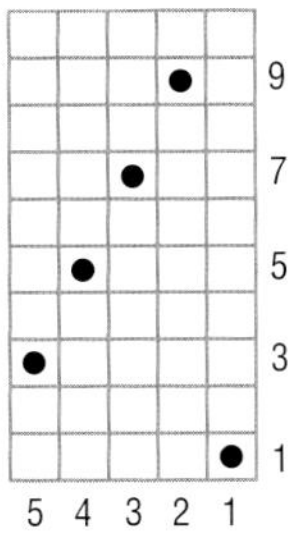
9
7
5
3
1
5 4 3 2 1

Left-Leaning Diagonal

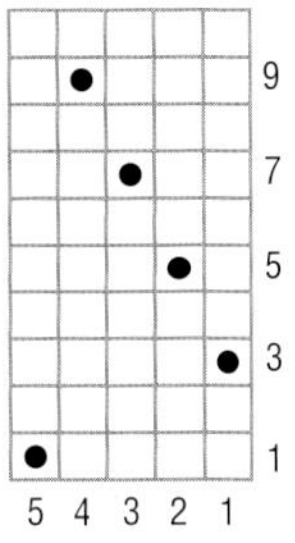
9
7
5
3
1
5 4 3 2 1

STITCH KEY

☐ Knit
RS: Knit stitch.
WS: Purl stitch.

● Purl
RS: Purl stitch.
WS: Knit stitch.

Start Diagonal Pattern

Work in est center front rib patt on 22 sts, sm, work in Left-leaning Diagonal patt on 30 (35, 40) sts, sm, work in Right-leaning Diagonal patt on 40 (45, 50) sts, sm. Starting on second st of Left-leaning Diagonal patt to preserve symmetry on back centerline, work in Left-leaning Diagonal patt on 40 (45, 50) sts, sm, work in Right-leaning Diagonal patt on rem 29 (34, 39) sts, sm.

Rep this established patt for 19 more rnds.

Next row: Work first 46 (51, 56) sts in est patt. BO next 11 sts for armhole, work next 69 (79, 89) sts in patt, BO next 11 sts for armhole, work in patt to next m, sm, and work until 1 st before BO sts. Set work aside. Front has 70 (80, 90) sts. Back has 69 (79, 89) sts.

SLEEVES (Make 2)

With dpns, CO 67, (77, 87) sts, pm, and join to work in the rnd.

Rnd 1: P2, (k2, p2) 4 times, pm, work in Seed Rib for 24 (29, 34) sts, pm, work to end in Seed Rib, pm.

Rnds 2–5: Rep rnd 1.

Rnd 6: P2, (k2, p2) 4 times, sm, work in Left-leaning Diagonal for 24 (29, 34) sts, pm, work to end in Right-leaning Diagonal, sm.

Rep rnd 6 48 more times.

Next rnd: P2, (k2, p2) 4 times, sm, work in diagonal as established on 19 (24, 29) sts, BO next 11 sts, work to end in established patt. Break off yarn—56 (66, 76) sts.

Make second sleeve as for first.

Join Sleeve to Body

Beg to the left of the BO sleeve sts, ktog first st of sleeve with last st of front body, pm, work sleeve sts onto circular needle until 1 st rem, k rem st tog with first st of back body, pm, work body sts in established patt until 1 st rem before second sleeve armhole BO.

Join Second Sleeve to Body

Beg to the left of the BO sleeve sts, k first st tog with last st of back body, pm, work rem sleeve sts onto circular needle until 1 st rem, k rem st tog with first st of front body, pm, work to end of rnd—247 (287, 327) total sts.

Work rnds in established patt, dec before and after the markers every other row 0 (4, 8) times and every 4 rows 6 times—199 (207, 215) total sts, front has 58 (60, 62) sts, back has 57 (59, 61) sts, each sleeve has 42 (44, 46) sts.

DIVIDE FOR V-NECK WITH CABLE SPLIT

Beg on next even numbered rnd of Diagonal patt and work first 8 sts of center front rib panel, place next 3 sts on a st holder held in front of work, k2tog, k1, turn, and end knitting in the round.

Note: *Although work will be turned at every row hereafter, it will be necessary to continue on circular needles at this point to avoid distorting the neckline.*

Next row, starting at left front neck edge (WS): Sl1, p1, work in patt to end, place 3 sts on holder back on needle, p2tog, p1, turn.

Next row, starting at right front neck edge (RS): Sl1 and work in established patt to end.

Dec Row, starting at right front neck edge (WS): Sl1, work in patt for 9 sts, p2tog, work in established patt to last 12 sts, p1, sl1, psso, work to end of row, finishing at the right front neck edge.

SPLIT CABLE FOR ARM CUTOUT

Starting at right front neck edge (RS): Beg on an odd number rnd of the diagonal patt, work first 6 sts of sleeve rib in patt, place next 3 sts on holder held in front of work, k2tog, k1, turn.

RIGHT FRONT

Change to straight needles. Work 50 (52, 54) sts in est patt—only on the sts between the arm cutout and neckline.

Dec Row (WS): Sl1, work in est patt until 12 sts rem, sl1, p1, psso, cont in est patt to end.

Next row (RS): Work in est patt.

Continue in est patt, rep Dec row 14 (16, 18) times, AT THE SAME TIME, dec 1 st outside armhole rib border every row 6 times, AT THE SAME TIME, when 31 sts rem, dec 1 st outside of armhole rib border until 20 sts rem.

Work in established patt until piece measures 7½ (8½, 10)"/19 (21.6, 25) cm from armhole BO, ending on RS.

Place first 8 sts of sleeve on a st holder. Place rem 12 sts (next to neckline) on a separate st holder. Break yarn.

BACK

(RS): Attach yarn to sts on holder at first sleeve cable split and k1, k2tog. From holder, cont across back in est patt to rib of second sleeve, work first 6 sts of sleeve rib in patt, place next 3 sts on a st holder held in front of work, k2tog, k1, turn work. Change to straight needles, and work only on back 97 (101, 105) sts.

Dec Row (RS and WS): Work arm cutout rib border in established patt, dec 1 st, work in est patt until 1 st rem before next arm cutout rib border, dec 1 st, cont in est arm cutout rib border.

Repeat dec row 5 more times—85 (89, 93) sts.

Sl first st of every row, and cont to work rem back sts in est patt between arm cutouts for 14 (18, 22) rows.

Back Neck Shaping (Short Rows)

Row 1 (RS): Work 8 sts, k2tog, work 17 sts, w/t.

Even rows 2 and 4 (WS): Work even in patt to end.

Row 3 (RS): Work 8 sts, k2tog, work 12 sts, w/t.

Row 5: Work 8 sts, k2tog, work 12 sts, w/t.

Even rows 6, 8, 10, 12, and 14: Work even to last 10 sts, p2tog, work in patt to end at arm cutout.

Row 7: Work 8 sts, k2tog, work 9 sts, w/t.

Row 9: Work 8 sts, k2tog, work 6 sts, w/t.

Row 11: Work 8 sts, k2tog, work 3 sts, w/t.

Row 13: Work 8 sts, w/t.

Row 15: Work row, incorporating all wraps.

Row 16 (WS): Work 8 sts, p2tog, work next 17 sts, w/t.

Odd rows 17 and 19 (RS): Work to end in patt.

Row 18 (WS): Work 8 sts, p2tog, work 12 sts, w/t.

Row 20: Work 8 sts, p2tog, work 12 sts, w/t.

Odd rows 21, 23, 25, 27, and 29: Work 8 sts, dec 1, work to end in patt.

Row 22: Work 8 sts, p2tog, work 9 sts, w/t.

Row 24: Work 8 sts, p2tog, work 6 sts, w/t.

Row 26: Work 8 sts, p2tog, work 3 sts, w/t.

Row 28: Work 8 sts, w/t.

Row 29: Work row in patt, incorporating all wraps.

Work even in est patt until piece measures 7½ (8, 10)"/19 (20.3, 25) cm from armhole BO.

Next row: Work 8 sts, place on st holder, BO sts to last 8 sts, place last 8 sts on st holder. Break yarn.

LEFT FRONT

Attach yarn at second sleeve cable split sts on holder.

On straight needles, k1, k2tog from holder, and continue to right side of neckline in est patt. Knit only on sts between the arm cutout and neckline.

Dec row (WS): Work 10 sts in patt; p2tog, continue in patt.

Continue in est patt, rep Dec row 14 (16, 18) times, AT THE SAME TIME, dec 1 st outside armhole rib border every row 6 times, AT THE SAME TIME, when 31 sts rem, dec 1 st outside of armhole rib border until 20 sts rem.

Work even on rem 20 sts until piece measures 7½ (8½, 10)"/19 (21.6, 25) cm from armhole BO, ending on RS.

Place 8 sts of sleeve on a st holder. To form back collar, work on the rem 12 sts until piece measures 12 (12¼, 12½)"/31 (31, 32) cm from the shoulder bindoffs.

Being careful not to twist sts, graft these 12 sts to the corresponding 12 sts on the opposite shoulder.

FINISHING

On both sleeves, graft front armhole ribbing to back armhole ribbing. Sew collar band to back, easing as necessary.

Sew underarms. Weave in ends.

ICE QUEEN SCHEMATIC

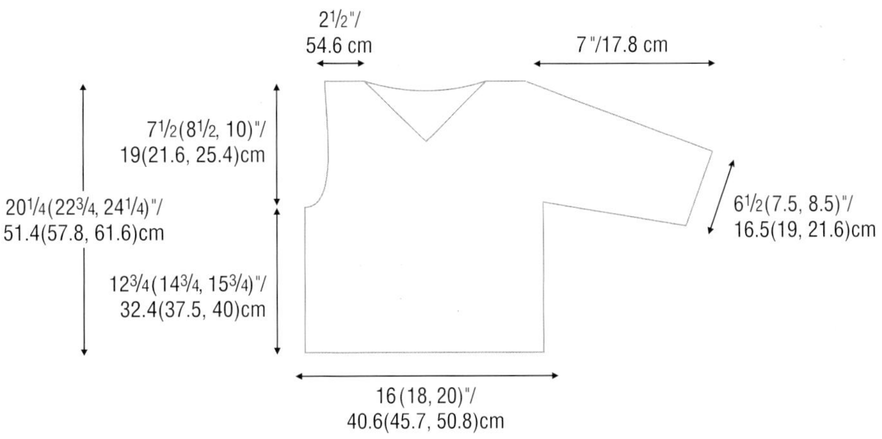

2½"/
54.6 cm
7"/17.8 cm
7½(8½, 10)"/
19(21.6, 25.4)cm
20¼(22¾, 24¼)"/
51.4(57.8, 61.6)cm
12¾(14¾, 15¾)"/
32.4(37.5, 40)cm
6½(7.5, 8.5)"/
16.5(19, 21.6)cm
16(18, 20)"/
40.6(45.7, 50.8)cm

CHAPTER 3

Wintry Lace

ATHENA

MELISSA WEHRLE

Athena can turn any knitter into a goddess. This tunic made of spun silk and light mohair is fit for heavenly royalty. The majestic braided belt mimics the architecture and style of ancient Greece.

THIS PROJECT WAS KNIT WITH:

Yarn A: Laines Du Nord Mulberry Silk (100% silk; 136 yd/50 g): 5 (5, 6, 6, 7, 7, 7) skeins, Natural (82)

Yarn B: Habu Textiles A-73 1/12 Silk Mohair Kusa (60% mohair, 40% silk; 186 yd/ 0.5 oz): 1 skein Natural

PATTERN NOTES

A two-stitch Selvedge pattern is worked at each side throughout at armholes and is included in the stitch counts.

Full-fashion decreases and increases are made only on the front of the tunic.

SPECIAL ABBREVIATIONS

DL: drop yo loop from previous row

PATTERN STITCHES

ARMHOLE SELVEDGE STITCH

Row 1 (RS): K1, p1, work to last 2 sts, p1, k1.

Row 2 (WS): P.

Row 3: Sl1 wyib, p1, work to last 2 sts, p1, sl1 wyib.

Rep rows 2 and 3.

INSTRUCTIONS

BACK

With 3.75 mm needles and Yarn A, CO 94 (101, 106, 112, 118, 123, 129) sts.

Beg with a WS row, work 3 rows in St st.

Change to 4.0 mm needles and work 10 (10, 10, 12, 12, 14, 14) rows in St st.

Dec Row (RS): K1, ssk, work to last 3 sts, k2tog, k1.

Rep dec row every 6 rows 7 (8, 8, 8, 8, 8, 8) times more, then every 4 rows 4 times—70 (75, 80, 86, 92, 97, 103) sts rem.

Work even until back measures 11½ (12½, 12½, 12¾, 13, 13¼, 13¼)"/29 (32, 32, 32, 33, 34, 34) cm from CO, ending with a WS row.

Inc Row (RS): Kfb, work to last 2 sts, kfb, k1.

SKILL LEVEL

Intermediate

SIZES

2XS (XS, S, M, L, XL, 2XL)
30 (32, 34, 36, 38, 40, 42)"/
76 (81, 86, 91, 97, 102, 107) cm
Shown in size S

FINISHED MEASUREMENTS

Chest: 29 (31, 33, 35, 37, 39, 41)"/ 74 (79, 84, 89, 94, 99, 104) cm

Length: 24 (24½, 25, 25½, 26, 26½, 26¾)"/61 (62, 64, 65, 66, 67, 68) cm

MATERIALS AND TOOLS

Yarn

Color A: 680 (680, 816, 816, 952, 952, 952) yd/622 (622, 746, 746, 871, 871, 871) m of light worsted weight yarn, 100% silk, in natural

Color B: 186 yd/170 m of worsted weight yarn, 60% mohair, 40% silk, in natural

Needles

3.75 mm (size 5 U.S.) straight
4.0 mm (size 6 U.S.) straight
3.75 mm (size F-5 U.S.) crochet hook
or size to obtain gauge

Notions

Two stitch markers
Tapestry needle

GAUGE

22 sts and 28 rows = 4"/10.2 cm in St st with 4.0 mm needles

Always take time to check your gauge.

Rep inc row every 6 rows 3 times more, then every 8 rows 1 time—80 (85, 90, 96, 102, 107, 113) sts.

Work even until back measures 16¾ (18, 18, 18¼, 18½, 19, 19)"/43 (46, 46, 46, 47, 48, 48) cm from CO, ending with a WS row.

Armhole Shaping

All Sizes:

BO 5 (5, 6, 6, 7, 7, 7) sts at beg of next 2 rows.

Dec Row 1 (RS): K1, p1, k1, k2tog, work to last 5 sts, ssk, k1, p1, k1.

Dec Row 2 (WS): P3, ssp, work to last 5 sts, p2tog, p3.

Dec Row 3 (RS): Sl1 wyib, p1, k1, k2tog, work to last 5, ssk, k1, p1, sl1 wyib.

Size 2XS:

Rep dec row 2 one time—62 sts.

Sizes XS and (S):

Rep dec row 3 every RS row 2 (3) times—65 (66) sts.

Sizes M (L, XL, and 2XL):

Rep dec rows 2 and 3 one time more, then rep dec row 3 every RS row 2 (3, 4, 5) times—70 (72, 75, 79) sts.

All Sizes:

Work even, working 2 Selvedge sts at each edge, until armhole measures 6¾ (7, 7¼, 7¼, 7½, 7½, 7¾)"/17 (18, 18, 18, 19, 19, 20) cm, ending with a WS row.

Back Neck Shaping

Work 10 (10, 10, 12, 12, 13, 15) sts and place remaining sts on holder.

Next row (WS): P1, p2tog, work to end of row. BO remaining 9 (9, 9, 11, 11, 12, 14) sts.

Reattach yarn, keeping center 42 (45, 46, 46, 48, 49, 49) sts on holder and work to end.

Next row (WS): Work across to last 3 sts, ssp, p1.

Work 1 row even.

BO rem 9 (9, 9, 11, 11, 12, 14) sts.

FRONT

With 3.75 mm needles and Yarn A, CO 94 (101, 106, 112, 118, 123, 129) sts. Beg with a WS row, work 3 rows in St st.

Change to 4.0 mm needles and work 10 (10, 10, 12, 12, 14, 14) rows in St st.

Dec Row 1: K1, ssk, work to last 3 sts, k2tog, k1.

Rep dec row 1 every 6th row 7 (8, 8, 8, 8, 8, 8) times more.

Dec Row 2: K19 (20, 20, 22, 24, 25, 26) sts, pm, k2tog, work across to last 21 (22, 22, 24, 26, 27, 28) sts, ssk, pm, k19 (20, 20, 22, 24, 25, 26) sts.

Rep dec row 2 every 4 rows 3 times more, sm as needed—70 (75, 80, 86, 92, 97, 103) sts.

Work even until front measures 11½ (12½, 12½, 12¾, 13, 13¼, 13¼)"/29 (32, 32, 32, 33, 34, 34) cm from CO, ending with a WS row.

Inc Row 1: Work across to first marker, sm, yo, work to 1 st before next m, yo, sm, work to end of row.

Rep inc row 1 every 4 rows 3 times more. Work 8 rows even.

Inc Row 2: Kfb, work to last 2 sts, kfb, k1—80 (85, 90, 96, 102, 107, 113) sts.

Work even until back measures 16¾ (17½, 18, 18¼, 18½, 19, 19)"/42.5 (44.5, 45.7, 46.4, 47, 48.3, 48.3) cm from CO, ending with a WS row.

Armhole Shaping

BO 5 (5, 6, 6, 7, 7, 7) sts at beg of next 2 rows.

Dec Row 1 (RS): K1, p1, k1, k2tog, work to last 5 sts, ssk, k1, p1, k1.

Next row (WS): P.

Dec Row 2 (RS): Sl1 wyib, p1, k1, k2tog, work to last 5, ssk, k1, p1, sl1 wyib.

Rep dec row 2 every 2 (2, 0, 0, 0, 0, 0) rows 1 (1, 0, 0, 0, 0, 0) time more. Work even until armhole measures 2¾ (3, 3, 3, 3, 3, 3)"/7(7.6, 7.6, 7.6, 7.6, 7.6, 7.6) cm.

Inc Row: Sl1 wyib, p1, kfb, work to last 4 sts, kfb, k1, p1, sl1 wyib.

Work inc row every other row 3 (4, 4, 4, 2, 2, 1) times more, then every 4 rows 5 (5, 5, 5, 7, 7, 8) times—82 (89, 94, 100, 104, 109, 115) sts.

Work even, working 2 selvedge sts at each edge, until armhole measures 6¾ (7, 7¼, 7¼, 7½, 7½, 7¾)"/17 (18, 18, 18, 19, 19, 20) cm, ending with a WS row.

Next row (WS): Work 9 (9, 9, 11, 11, 12, 14) sts in St st, work in p1, k1 rib to last 9 (9, 9, 11, 11, 12, 14), work in St st.

Next row (RS): BO all stitches in patt.

FINISHING

Block pieces to finished measurements. Sew shoulder and side seams. With crochet hook and Yarn A, work 1 row crochet edge finish on back neck only. Weave in ends.

Bottom Lace Trim

With 3.75 mm needles and Yarn B, CO 18 sts. Knit 1 row.

Set-up Row: K5, k2tog, k2, yo, k1, k2tog, yo, k2tog, k1, yo k3.

Row 1: Sl1, k2, yo, slip yo of previous row, k2, kfb, k3, sl next 2 sts to dpn and hold in front, k3, k2 from dpn, yo, k2tog, k1.

Row 2: CO 2 sts and BO 2 sts, k6, k2tog, yo, k2tog, k4, (k1, p1) into both yo loops together as if a single stitch, k3.

Row 3: Sl1, k1, k2tog, yo, k2tog, k10, yo, k2tog, k1.

Row 4: K5, (yo, k1) twice, k2tog, yo, k2tog, k3, yo, DL, k3.

Row 5: Sl1, k2, (k1, p1) into yo from previous row, k7, kfb, k1, kfb, k2, yo, k2tog, k1.

Row 6: CO 2 sts and BO 2 sts, k4, yo, k2, yo, k2tog, k1, yo, (k1, k2tog, yo, k2tog) twice, k2.

Row 7: Sl1, k2, yo, DL, k6, (yo, k2tog, k1) 4 times.

Row 8: K5, (yo, k2tog, k1) 3 times, yo, k2tog, k2, (k1, p1) into yo from previous row, k3.

Row 9: Sl1, k1, k2tog, yo, k2tog, k5, (yo, k2tog, k1) 4 times.

Row 10: CO 2 sts and BO 2 sts, k4, (yo, k1, k2tog) 3 times, yo, k2tog, k2, yo, DL, k3.

Row 11: Sl1, k2, (k1, p1) into yo of previous row, k6, (yo, k2tog, k1) 4 times.

Row 12: K5, (yo, k2tog, k1) 4 times, k2tog, yo, k2tog, k2.

Row 13: Sl1, k2, yo, DL, k6, (yo, k2tog, k1) 4 times.

Row 14: CO 2 sts and BO 2 sts, k4, (yo, k2tog, k1) 3 times, yo, k2tog, k2, (k1, p1) into yo of previous row, k3.

Row 15: Sl1, k1, k2tog, yo, k2tog, k5, (yo, k2tog, k1) 4 times.

Row 16: K5, (yo, k2tog, k1) 3 times, yo, k2tog, k2, yo, DL, k3.

Row 17: Sl1, k2, (k1, p1) into yo of previous row, k6, yo, (k2tog, k1) twice, (yo, k2tog, k1) twice.

Row 18: CO 2 sts and BO 2 sts, k4, yo, k2tog, k1, k2tog, yo, k2tog, k1, yo, k3, k2tog, yo, k2tog, k2.

Row 19: Sl1, k2, yo, DL, k7, yo, k2tog, k2 (yo, k2tog, k1) twice.

Row 20: K5, yo, (k2tog) twice, yo, k2tog, k1, yo, k5, (k1, p1) into yo of previous row, k3.

Row 21: Sl1, k1, k2tog, yo, k2tog, k7, (k2tog, k1) twice, yo, k2tog, k1.

Row 22: K5, k2tog, k2, yo, k1, k2tog, yo, k2tog, k1, yo, DL, k3.

Rep rows 1–22 until piece measures 34½ (36½, 38½, 40½, 43, 44½, 47)"/88 (93, 98, 103, 109, 113, 119) cm long or circumference of tunic's hem.

Seaming

Sew shoulder seams and side seams of tunic.

With Yarn B, sew ends of lace trim together and then sew lace to 3 rows above CO edge on inside of tunic.

Stitches will be hidden by rolled edge of tunic.

Belt Loops

With crochet hook and Yarn A, and leaving a long tail to sew into side seam, chain two 1"/2.5 cm-long belt loops (one for each side seam). Break off yarn, leaving a tail to sew into side seam. Sew each end of belt loop securely to each side seam 12 (12½, 12¾, 12¾, 13, 13¼, 13½)"/31 (32, 32, 32, 33, 34, 34) cm down from top of shoulder.

Belt

Cut 15 lengths of Yarn A 48 (48, 48, 50, 50, 52, 54)"/122 (122, 122, 127, 127, 132, 137) cm long or desired length for belt. Knot one end. Separate lengths of yarn into 3 sections of 5 strands each. Braid yarn to end and knot. Trim ends even.

ATHENA SCHEMATIC

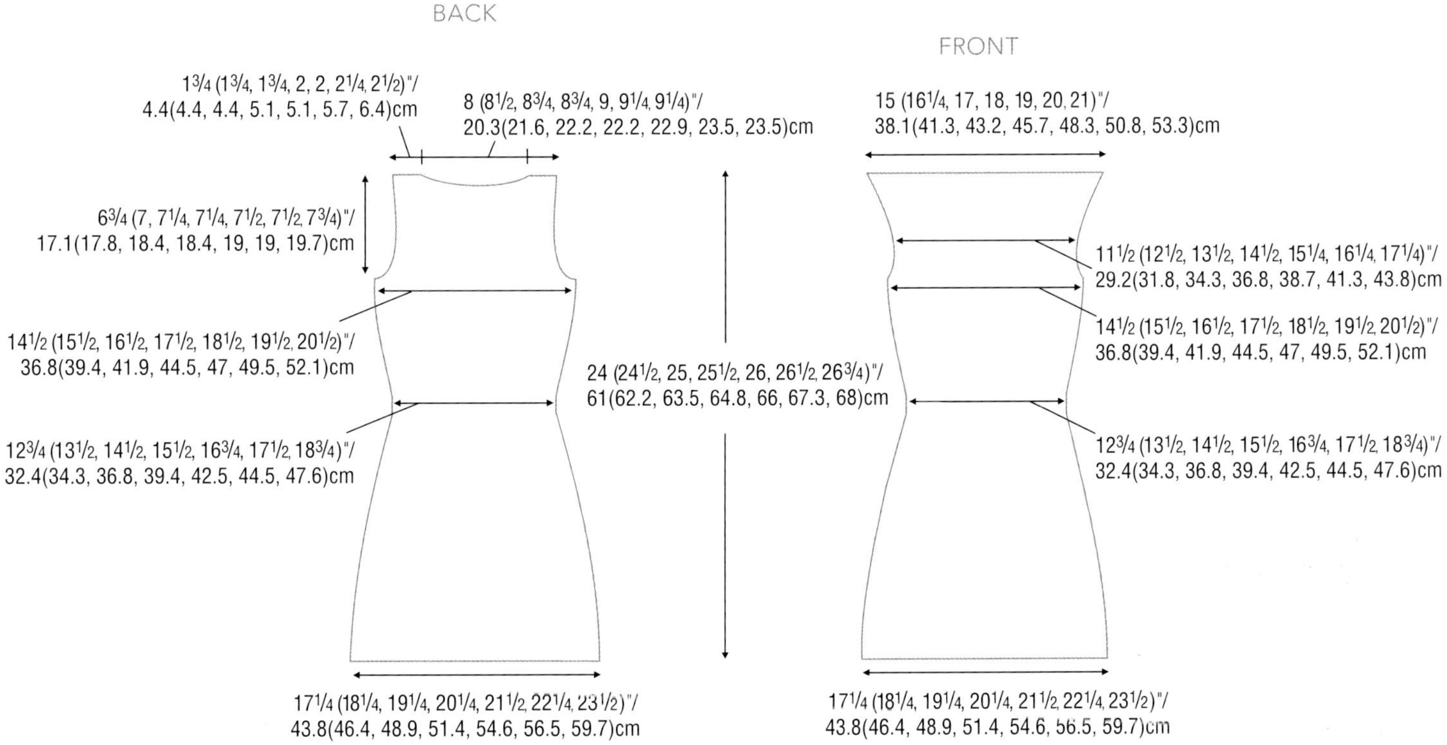
BACK
FRONT
1¾ (1¾, 1¾, 2, 2, 2¼, 2½)"/
4.4(4.4, 4.4, 5.1, 5.1, 5.7, 6.4)cm
8 (8½, 8¾, 8¾, 9, 9¼, 9¼)"/
20.3(21.6, 22.2, 22.2, 22.9, 23.5, 23.5)cm
15 (16¼, 17, 18, 19, 20, 21)"/
38.1(41.3, 43.2, 45.7, 48.3, 50.8, 53.3)cm
6¾ (7, 7¼, 7¼, 7½, 7½, 7¾)"/
17.1(17.8, 18.4, 18.4, 19, 19, 19.7)cm
11½ (12½, 13½, 14½, 15¼, 16¼, 17¼)"/
29.2(31.8, 34.3, 36.8, 38.7, 41.3, 43.8)cm
14½ (15½, 16½, 17½, 18½, 19½, 20½)"/
36.8(39.4, 41.9, 44.5, 47, 49.5, 52.1)cm
14½ (15½, 16½, 17½, 18½, 19½, 20½)"/
36.8(39.4, 41.9, 44.5, 47, 49.5, 52.1)cm
24 (24½, 25, 25½, 26, 26½, 26¾)"/
61(62.2, 63.5, 64.8, 66, 67.3, 68)cm
12¾ (13½, 14½, 15½, 16¾, 17½, 18¾)"/
32.4(34.3, 36.8, 39.4, 42.5, 44.5, 47.6)cm
12¾ (13½, 14½, 15½, 16¾, 17½, 18¾)"/
32.4(34.3, 36.8, 39.4, 42.5, 44.5, 47.6)cm
17¼ (18¼, 19¼, 20¼, 21½, 22¼, 23½)"/
43.8(46.4, 48.9, 51.4, 54.6, 56.5, 59.7)cm
17¼ (18¼, 19¼, 20¼, 21½, 22¼, 23½)"/
43.8(46.4, 48.9, 51.4, 54.6, 56.5, 59.7)cm

FALLING SNOW

SARAH HEINIGER

The lacy snow pattern of this winter white pullover is the perfect garment to wear for holiday parties, over jeans, with a skirt, over a plain tank, or with a frilly party shirt. The subtle shaping allows for a variety of uses and stylings.

SKILL LEVEL

Intermediate

SIZES

XS (S, M, L, XL)
30 (34, 38, 42, 46, 50)"/
76 (86, 97, 107, 117, 127) cm
Shown in size S

FINISHED MEASUREMENTS

Bust: 32 (34, 36, 38, 40)"/
81 (86, 91, 97, 102) cm
Collar to hem: 19 (19, 21, 21, 23)"/48 (48, 53, 53, 58) cm
Hips: 34 (36, 38, 40, 42)"/
86 (91, 97, 102, 107) cm

MATERIALS AND TOOLS

Yarn

170 (170, 340, 340, 340) yd/155 (155, 311, 311, 311) m worsted weight yarn, 70% silk, 30% mohair, in natural

Needles

5.0 mm (size 8 U.S.) circular, 32"/81 cm long
or size to obtain gauge

Notions

Stitch markers
Tapestry needle

GAUGE

16 sts and 8 rows = 4"/10.2 cm (4 pattern repeats wide and 2 tall), worked over Snowfall Lace pattern, blocked

Always take time to check your gauge.

THIS PROJECT WAS KNIT WITH:

Neighborhood Fiber Co Silk Mohair (70% silk, 30% mohair, 170 yd/0.5 oz): 1 (1, 2, 2, 2) skeins, Natural

PATTERN NOTES

When determining gauge, keep in mind that lace stretches quite a bit when blocked. It is very important to take your gauge from a blocked swatch.

INSTRUCTIONS

BODY

HEM FRILL

CO 14 sts on 5.0 mm needles. Work hem pattern set-up rnd, and then work Hem Frill patt rnds 1–6 24 (25, 26, 27, 28) times.

BO all stitches.

Sew CO and BO edges together with a backstitch.

Body

With circular needles, p/u and k167 (173, 179, 185, 191) sts along top straight edge of hem, pm (beg of rnd and center back), and join to knit in the rnd.

Work rnds 1–8 of Snowfall Lace pattern 20 (21, 22, 23, 24) times, including the 4 st pattern once at the end.

Next Rnd: Work 5 (5, 6, 7, 8) patt rep, pm, work 1 patt rep, pm (left side), work 10 (11, 11, 11, 12) patt rep, pm, work 1 patt rep, pm (right side), work to end of rnd.

There are 5 markers: 4 side markers (2 at the left side and 2 at the right side) and 1 marker at the back/end of rnd.

Next: Work patt rnds 2–8 1 (1, 2, 2, 3) times.

Next: Work patt rnds 1–7 1 time.

Waist Shaping

Dec Rnd: Work to first m, sm, k3, k2tog, k3, sm, work to next m, sm, k3, k2tog, k3, sm, work to end of row, and sm (7 sts between side m)—165 (171, 177, 183, 189) sts rem.

Next: Work patt rnds 1–5.

Next: Work patt rnd 6; rep dec rnd (6 sts between side m)—163 (169, 175, 181, 187) sts rem.

Next: Work patt rnds 7–8 and 1–3.

Next: Work patt rnd 4; repeat dec row (5 sts between side ms)—161 (167, 173, 179, 185) sts rem.

Next: Work patt rnds 5–8.

Inc Rnd: Work as for patt rnd 1 to m, sm, k4, kfb, sm, work to next m, sm, k4, kfb, sm, work to end of row—163 (169, 175, 181, 187) sts rem.

Rep inc rnd 2 more times on patt rnd 6 (8 sts between m)—7 (7, 8, 8, 9) total pattern repeats completed; 167 (173, 179, 185, 191) sts rem.

PATTERN STITCHES

HEM FRILL PATTERN

Multiple of 14 sts.

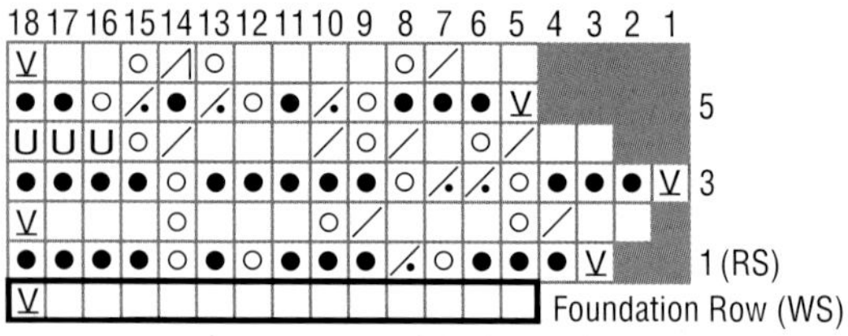
18 17 16 15 14 13 12 11 10 9 8 7 6 5 4 3 2 1
5
3
1 (RS)
Foundation Row (WS)

STITCH KEY

Highlighted Repeat

Knit
RS: Knit stitch
WS: Purl stitch

k2tog
RS: Knit 2 stitches together.
WS: Purl 2 stitches together.

k3tog
RS: Knit 3 stitches together.
WS: Purl 3 stitches together.

No Stitch Placeholder.

Cast on

Cast on

Purl
RS: Purl stitch.
WS: Knit stitch.

p2tog
RS: Purl 2 stitches together.
WS: Knit 2 stitches together.

slip wyif
RS: Slip 1 stitch as if to purl with yarn in front.
WS: Slip 1 stitch as if to purl with yarn in back.

yo
Yarn Over.

SNOWFALL LACE PATTERN

Multiple of 8 sts plus 5 sts.

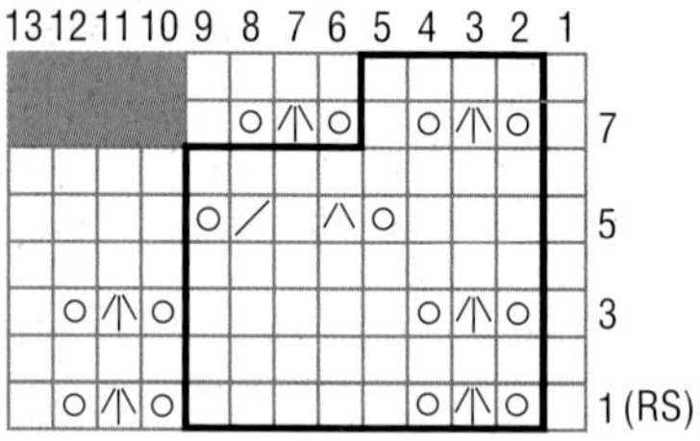
13 12 11 10 9 8 7 6 5 4 3 2 1
7
5
3
1 (RS)

STITCH KEY

Highlighted Repeat

Knit
RS: Knit
WS: Purl

k2tog
RS: Knit two stitches together as one stitch.

No Stitch Placeholder

sl1 k2tog, psso
RS: Slip 1, k2tog, pass slipped stitch over.

sl1, k, psso
RS: Slip 1, knit 1, pass slipped stitch over.

yo
Yarn Over.

Armhole and Neck Shaping

On next patt rnd 8, k to first m, remove marker, BO the 8 sts between m, sm, k to next m, remove m, BO the 8 sts between m, sm, k to end of row. Break yarn.

End of rnd m is now center back.

BACK

Beg working back and forth on back. Attach yarn at the right side of back and work patt row 1 (RS) on 75 (78, 81, 84, 87) sts (Back).

Place rem 75 (78, 81, 84, 87) sts (Front) on a st holder.

Next: Work patt rows 2–8 1 time.

Next: Work patt rows 1–8 0 (0, 1, 1, 2) times more, dec 1 st at each end on every p (WS) row.

Next (Patt Row 1): Work 26 (30, 34, 38, 42) sts, BO 8 center sts, work to end of row.

Cont to dec 1 st each side on every WS row, while AT THE SAME TIME dec on neck edges as follows.

BO 4 (4, 6, 6, 8) sts at beg of the next RS row (patt row 3), work to end.

Next row (WS): Dec 1 st each side, work to end.

Next row (RS): BO 2 (2, 4, 4, 6) sts at neck edge, work to end of row.

Next row (WS): Dec 1 st at each side, work to end.

Next row (RS): BO 2 (2, 4, 4, 6) sts at neck edge, work to end of row.

Cont to work in patt and work dec as follows.

Dec 1 st each side on the next and every row (every row, every other row, every other row, every 3 rows) and AT THE SAME TIME dec 1 st at the neck edge on every other row (every other row, every 3 rows, every 3 rows, every 4 rows) until 4 sts rem.

K4tog. BO remaining stitch.

Attach yarn to the right side of back at armhole BO.

Next row (patt row 3), dec as follows: K2tog at armhole edge (RS), work to end of row.

Next row (WS): BO 4 sts at beg of row, work to end of row.

Next row (RS): K2tog at armhole edge, work to end of row.

Next row (WS): BO 2 sts at neck edge, work to end of row.

Next row (RS): K2tog at armhole edge, work to end of row.

Next row (WS): BO 2 sts at neck edge, work to end of row.

Cont to work in patt and dec as follows. On the next and every row (every row, every other row, every other row, every 3 rows), k2tog at armhole edge while AT THE SAME TIME dec 1 st at neck edge every other row (every other row, every 3 rows, every 3 rows, every 4 rows) until 4 sts rem.

K4tog. BO remaining sts.

FRONT

Move sts on holder to needles.

Attach yarn at the right side of the front piece and work patt row 1 (RS).

Next row (patt row 2 and dec row) (WS): P2tog at each side, work to end.

Next row (patt row 3) (RS): Work 35 stitches, BO center 10 sts, work to end of row.

Next row (patt row 4) (WS): Dec 1 st, work to end of row (neckline edge).

Next row (patt row 5) (RS): BO 4 sts at beg of next row (neck edge), work to end of row.

Next row (WS): Dec 1 st, work to end of row.

Next row (row 7) (RS): BO 2 sts at neck edge, work to end of row.

Next row (WS): Dec 1 st, work to end of row.

Next row (RS): BO 2 sts at neck edge, work to end of row.

Cont to work in pattern and decrease as follows.

Dec 1 st each side on the next and every row (every row, every other row, every other row, every 3 rows), while AT THE SAME TIME dec 1 st at neck edge every other row (every other row, every 3 rows, every 3 rows, every 4 rows) until 4 sts rem.

K4tog. BO remaining stitch.

Attach yarn to RS of left front.

Next row: Work patt row 5.

Next row (patt row 6) (WS): BO 4 sts, work to end of row.

Next row (patt row 7) (RS): Dec 1 st, work to end of row.

Next row (patt row 8) (WS): BO 2 sts at neck edge, work to end of row.

Next row (patt row 1) (RS): Dec 1 st, work to end of row.

Next row (patt row 2) (WS): BO 2 sts at neck edge, work to end of row.

Cont to work in patt and decrease as follows.

Dec 1 st at each side on the next and every row (every row, every other row, every other row, every 3 rows) while AT THE SAME TIME dec 1 st at neck edge every other row (every other row, every 3 rows, every 3 rows, every 4 rows) until 4 sts rem.

K4tog. BO remaining stitch.

SLEEVES (Make 2)

Cuff

With straight needles, CO 14 sts. Work in Hem Frill patt, working rep 7 (8, 8, 9, 9) times.

BO all sts.

Sleeve Cap

P/u and k24 (33, 33, 42, 42) sts along top (straight) edge. Work back and forth in Snowfall Lace patt.

Row 2 (WS): BO 3 (4, 4, 6, 6) sts at beg of row, work to end.

Row 3 (RS): BO 3 (4, 4, 6, 6) sts at beg of row, work to end.

Rows 4–5: Work in patt.

Next WS row: Dec 1 st at each edge and every 4 (4, 4, 5, 6) rows until 18 (18, 18, 28, 28) sts rem, then on every other row until 8 (8, 8, 14 14) sts rem.

Next: Work 3 (3, 3, 5, 5) rows in pattern. BO all sts.

FINISHING

Block all pieces to measurements on diagram. Sew sleeves to body with a backstitch along dec edges of sleeve and body. The 8 (8, 8, 14, 14) sts along the top edge of each sleeve become part of the collar.

Collar

Beg at front seam, p/u and k 51 (55, 59, 63, 67) sts along front, 8 (8, 8, 14, 14) sts along shoulder, 51 (55, 59, 63, 67) sts along back, and 8 (8, 8, 14, 14) sts along shoulder—118 (126, 134, 142, 150) sts rem.

Work in garter st for 3 rows.

Work picot border as follows.

BO 3 sts, *sl1 st on RH needle back to LH needle, CO 3 sts, BO 6 sts*, repeat between * to end.

Weave in ends.

FALLING SNOW SCHEMATIC

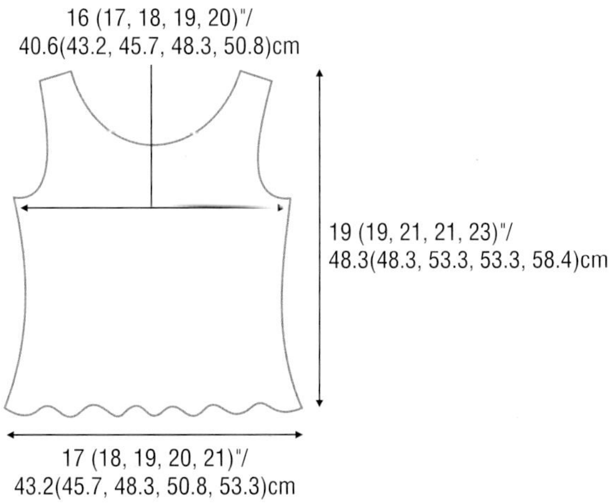
16 (17, 18, 19, 20)"/
40.6(43.2, 45.7, 48.3, 50.8)cm
19 (19, 21, 21, 23)"/
48.3(48.3, 53.3, 53.3, 58.4)cm
17 (18, 19, 20, 21)"/
43.2(45.7, 48.3, 50.8, 53.3)cm

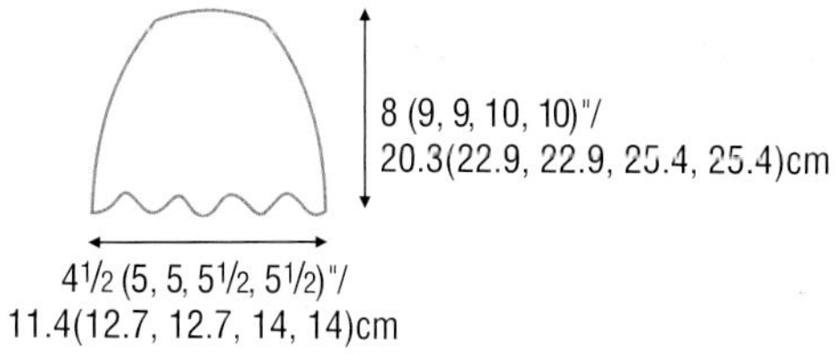
8 (9, 9, 10, 10)"/
20.3(22.9, 22.9, 25.4, 25.4)cm
4½ (5, 5, 5½, 5½)"/
11.4(12.7, 12.7, 14, 14)cm

NICOLE CARDIGAN

ANDREA TUNG

This elegant cardigan can be easily worn with fitted jeans or a fiery floral print dress. Wear it open or closed with a jeweled vintage brooch. It features an intriguing lace panel design on each front side and along the sleeves.

THIS PROJECT WAS KNIT WITH:

Fable Handknit Cotton Tencel
(50% pima cotton, 50% tencel;
108 yd/50 g): 8 (8, 8, 10) skeins,
Natural (01)

PATTERN STITCH

LACE PANEL

Multiple of 21 sts.

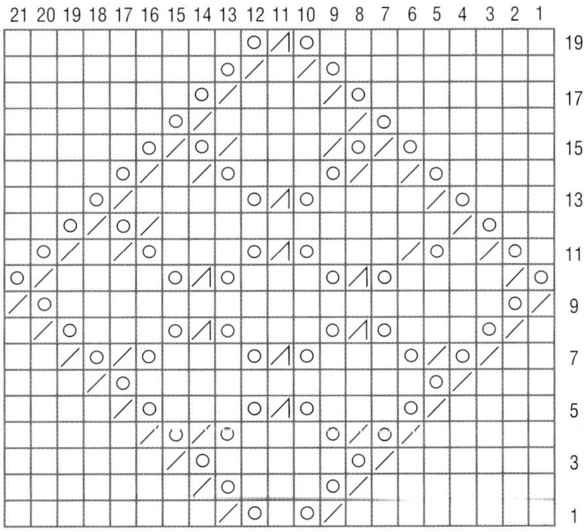
21 20 19 18 17 16 15 14 13 12 11 10 9 8 7 6 5 4 3 2 1
19
17
15
13
11
9
7
5
3
1

STITCH KEY

Knit
RS: Knit
WS: Purl

k2tog
RS: Knit 2 stitches together.
WS: Purl 2 stitches together.

k3tog
RS: Knit 3 stitches together.
WS: Purl 3 stitches together.

yo
Yarn Over.

SKILL LEVEL

Easy

SIZES

S (M, L, XL)
34 (36, 38, 40)"/86 (91, 97, 102) cm
Shown in size S

FINISHED MEASUREMENTS

Length: 21 (21½, 22, 22½)"/ 53 (55, 55, 57) cm
Bust and hem width: 34 (36, 38, 40)"/86 (91, 97, 102) cm
Shoulders: 14 (14½, 15, 15½)"/ 36 (37, 38, 39) cm

MATERIALS AND TOOLS

Yarn

864 (864, 864, 1080) yd/790 (790, 790, 988) m of worsted weight yarn, 50% pima cotton, 50% tencel, in natural

Needles

4.0 mm (size 6 U.S.) circular, 24"/61 cm long
4.0 mm (size 6 U.S.) dpns
or size to obtain gauge

Notions

Stitch markers
Stitch holders
Tapestry needle

GAUGE

20 sts and 26 rows = 4"/ 10.2 cm in St st

Always take time to check your gauge.

LEFT FRONT

CO 41 (44, 47, 50) sts. Work in k1, p1 rib for 1½"/3.8 cm.

Work in St st until piece measures 5"/12.7 cm from CO.

Beg to work lace panels as follows.

Row 1 (RS): K13 (16, 19, 22), pm, work Lace Panel patt on 21 sts, pm, k7.

Row 2 (WS): P7, pm, work Lace Panel patt on 21 sts, pm, p13 (16, 19, 22).

After lace panel is complete, work even for 7 rows. Repeat, working 3 lace panels.

AT THE SAME TIME, when piece measures 11"/28 cm from CO, beg armhole shaping.

Armhole Shaping

BO 4 (5, 5, 6) sts, work to end. P 1 row.

Work decreases as follows.

Row 1: K3, k2tog tbl, k to end of row.

Row 2: P to last 5 sts, p2tog tbl, p3—35 (37, 40, 42) sts rem.

Dec 1 st every row at side edge 3 (4, 5, 5) times—32 (33, 35, 37) sts rem.

Neck Shaping

Row 1 (WS): BO 5 sts, p to end of row.

Row 2: K.

Rows 3–4: BO 2 sts, p to end of row.

Dec 1 st (k2tog on RS, p2tog on WS) at neck edge 7 (8, 10, 11) times—18 (19, 18, 19) sts rem.

Work until piece measures 19½ (20, 20½, 21)"/50 (51, 52, 53) cm from CO.

Shoulder Shaping

Beg short row shoulder shaping.

Row 1–2: work to last 6 sts, W/T.

Row 3–4: Work to last 12 sts, W/T.

Row 5: Work all sts, picking up wraps.

RIGHT FRONT

Work same as left front, reversing directions.

BACK

CO 84 (90, 94, 100) sts. Work in k1, p1 rib for 1½"/3.8 cm. Work in St st until piece measures 13"/33 cm from CO.

Armhole Shaping

BO 4 (5, 5, 6) sts at beg of next 2 rows.

Purl 1 row.

Work decreases as follows:

Row 1: K3, k2tog tbl, k to last 5 sts, k2tog, k3.

Row 2: P3, p2tog, p to last 5 sts, p2tog, p3.

74 (78, 82, 86) sts rem.

Dec 1 st on each end of every row, 3 (4, 5, 5) times.

66 (68, 70, 74) sts rem.

Work until pieces measures 19½ (20, 20 ½, 21)"/49.5 (50.8, 52, 53.3) cm from CO.

Shoulder Shaping

Beg short row shoulder shaping.

Row 1–2: work to last 6 sts, W/T.

Rows 3–4: work to last 12 sts, W/T.

Row 5: work all sts, picking up wraps.

Neck Shaping

P18 (19, 18, 19), BO 30 (30, 34, 36) sts, p18 (19, 18, 19).

Place rem 18 (19, 18, 19) sts on each side on holders.

SLEEVES (Make 2)

Sleeve Hem

CO 51 (53, 57, 61) sts. Work in k1, p1 rib for ½"/1.3 cm.

Sleeve Shaping

Work in St st for 10 rows.

Beg to work lace panel as follows.

Row 1: K15 (16, 18, 20), pm, work Lace Panel patt on 21 sts, pm, k15 (16, 18, 20).

Row 2: P15 (16, 18, 20), pm, work Lace Panel patt on 21 sts, pm, p15 (16, 18, 20).

After lace panel is complete, work 5 rows even. Repeat, working 3 lace panels.

AT THE SAME TIME, inc 1 st on each side every 14th row 2 times, and then every 16 rows 3 times—61 (63, 67, 71) sts.

Work until pieces measure 12½ (12½, 12½, 13)"/32 (32, 32, 33) cm from CO.

Cap Shaping

BO 4 (4, 5, 6) sts at beg of the next 2 rows—53 (55, 57, 59) sts rem.

Work decreases as follows.

Row 1: K3, k2tog tbl, work to last 5 sts, k2tog, k3.

Row 2: P3, p2tog, work to last 5 sts, p2tog tbl, p3.

Dec 1 st each side on every row 3 (3, 3, 3) times—43 (45, 47, 49) sts rem. Dec 1 st each side on every other row 9 (9, 9, 9) times.

Dec 1 st each side every 4th row 1 (2, 3, 4) times.

BO 3 sts at beg of next 4 rows.

BO rem 11 sts.

FINISHING

Block to measurements. Join shoulders using 3-needle BO. Sew in sleeves and side seams.

Front Rib Bands

P/u 87 sts along center front edge.
Row 1: K1, *p1, k1, rep from * to last st, k1.

Row 2: P1, *k1, p1, rep from * to last st, p1.

Repeat rows 1 and 2 one more time. BO in rib.

Neck Rib

Pick up 18 sts on holder for right front neck, 39 sts along back neck, and 18 sts on holder for left front.

Row 1: K1, *p1, k1, rep from * to last st, k1.

Row 2: P1, *k1, p1, rep from * to last st, p1.

Repeat rows 1 and 2 one more time. BO in rib.

Weave in loose ends.

NICOLE CARDIGAN SCHEMATIC

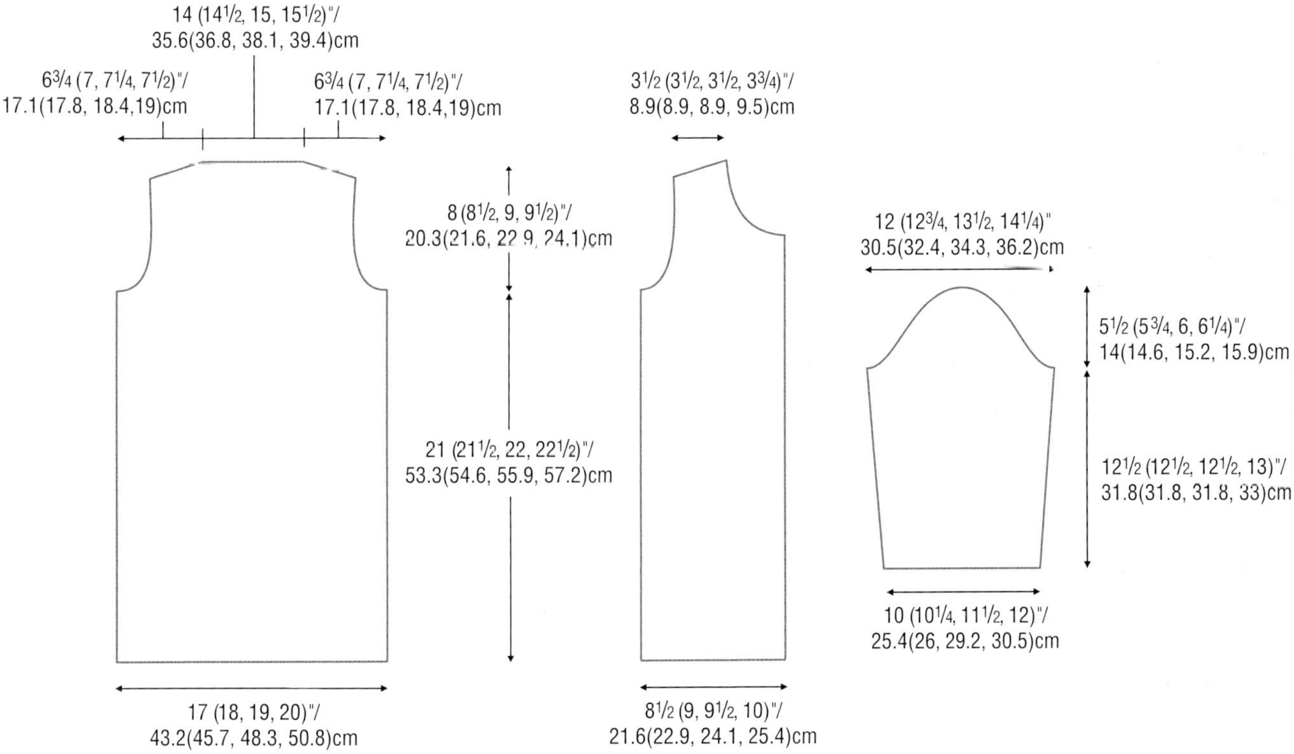
14 (14 1/2, 15, 15 1/2)"/
35.6(36.8, 38.1, 39.4)cm
6 3/4 (7, 7 1/4, 7 1/2)"/
17.1(17.8, 18.4,19)cm
6 3/4 (7, 7 1/4, 7 1/2)"/
17.1(17.8, 18.4,19)cm
8 (8 1/2, 9, 9 1/2)"/
20.3(21.6, 22.9, 24.1)cm
21 (21 1/2, 22, 22 1/2)"/
53.3(54.6, 55.9, 57.2)cm
17 (18, 19, 20)"/
43.2(45.7, 48.3, 50.8)cm
3 1/2 (3 1/2, 3 1/2, 3 3/4)"/
8.9(8.9, 8.9, 9.5)cm
8 1/2 (9, 9 1/2, 10)"/
21.6(22.9, 24.1, 25.4)cm
12 (12 3/4, 13 1/2, 14 1/4)"
30.5(32.4, 34.3, 36.2)cm
5 1/2 (5 3/4, 6, 6 1/4)"/
14(14.6, 15.2, 15.9)cm
12 1/2 (12 1/2, 12 1/2, 13)"/
31.8(31.8, 31.8, 33)cm
10 (10 1/4, 11 1/2, 12)"/
25.4(26, 29.2, 30.5)cm

SNOW PRINCESS DRESS

MELISSA WEHRLE

Any little girl will feel like a princess in this textured cashmere dress. The demure lace pattern on the skirt continues to the sleeves. Knit this beautiful dress for a special occasion, a holiday, or even to play dress-up. This garment will be cherished as a family heirloom for years to come.

SKILL LEVEL

Intermediate

SIZES

2 (4, 6, 8, 10)
Shown in size 6

FINISHED MEASUREMENTS

Chest: 22 (24, 25, 26, 27)"/ 55 (61, 64, 66, 69) cm

Length: 23 (24½, 25, 26, 27½)"/ 58 (62, 64, 66, 70) cm

MATERIALS AND TOOLS

Yarn

600 (800, 800, 1000, 1000) yd/549 (732, 732, 914, 914) m of DK weight yarn, 100% cashmere, in pearl

Needles

3.75 mm (size 5 U.S.) straight
4.0 mm (size 6 U.S.) straight
3.75 mm (size 5 U.S.) circular, 16"/41 cm long
3.7 5mm (size F-5 U.S.) crochet hook
or size to obtain gauge

Notions

Two stitch holders
Tapestry needle
2 yards/183 cm 1½"/3.8 cm-wide satin ribbon

GAUGE

24 sts and 28 rows = 4"/10.2 cm in St st with 3.75 mm needles
25 sts and 28 rows = 4"/10.2 cm in Lace pattern on 4.0 mm needles

Always take time to check your gauge.

THIS PROJECT WAS KNIT WITH:

Black Pearl Yarns "Pure Cashmere" (100% Cashmere; 200 yd/2 oz): 3 (4, 4, 5, 5) skeins, Jasmine Pearl

3

PATTERN NOTES

One selvedge stitch is worked at each side throughout on body and sleeve and is included in the stitch counts. This allows for easier seaming, especially in the lace areas.

PATTERN STITCHES

LACE PATTERN

Multiple of 10 sts + 1.

Row 1 (and all other WS rows): P.

Rows 2, 4, 6, 8 (RS): K1, *yo, k3, sl1, k2tog, psso, k3, yo, k1; rep from *.

Rows 10, 12, 14, 16: K2tog, *k3, yo, k1, yo, k3, sl1, k2tog, psso; rep from * to last 7 sts, and end k3, yo, k1, yo, ssk.

Rep rows 1–16.

INSTRUCTIONS

BACK

With 4.0 mm straight needles, CO 83 (93, 103, 113, 123) sts. Beg with a WS row and working 1 selvedge st at each side throughout, work in Lace patt for 1½ (1½, 1½, 1½, 2, 2)"/3.8 (3.8, 3.8, 3.8, 5, 5) cm ending with a WS row.

Dec row (RS): Cont to work in patt, k1, ssk, work to last 3 sts in patt, k2tog, k1.

Rep dec row every 16 (12, 10, 8, 8) rows 1 (5, 6, 10, 4) more times, then every 14 (10, 8, 6, 6) rows 6 (4, 5, 3, 11) times—67 (73, 79, 85, 91) sts.

Work even in Lace patt until back measures 16½ (17, 17, 17, 17)"/42 (43, 43, 43, 43) cm from CO.

Change to 3.75 mm straight needles and St st, work even until back measures 18½ (19, 19, 20¼, 21)"/ 47 (48, 48, 51, 53) cm from CO, ending with a WS row.

Armhole Shaping

BO 5 (5, 5, 6, 7) sts at beg of next 2 rows.

Dec row: K1, k2tog, work to last 3 sts, ssk, k1.

Repeat dec row every row 3 (3, 4, 4, 5) more times—49 (55, 59, 63, 65) sts.

Work even until back measures 22½ (24, 24½, 26, 27)"/57.2(61, 62.2, 66, 68.6) cm from CO, ending with a WS row.

LACE PATTERN

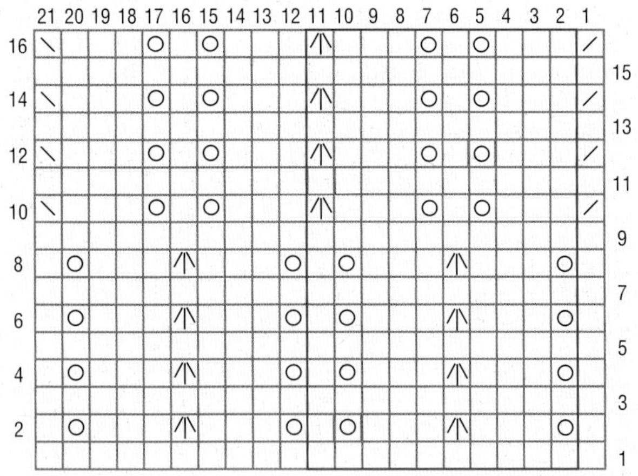

STITCH KEY

Knit
RS: Knit
WS: Purl

K2tog
Knit 2 together

Sl1, K2tog, psso
Slip 1, knit 2 together, pass slipped stitch over

ssk
Slip, slip, knit

Repeat

yo
Yarn over

Back Neck and Shoulder Shaping

BO 5 (6, 6, 6, 6) sts at armhole edge, k5 (5, 6, 6, 6) sts, and place rem 38 (42, 46, 50, 52) sts on holder.

Next row (WS): P1, p2tog, work to end of row. BO rem 5 (5, 6, 6, 6) sts.

Attach yarn at other side at neck edge, keeping center 27 (31, 33, 37, 39) sts on holder.

Work one row even.

Next row (WS): BO 5 (6, 6, 6, 6) sts at armhole edge, work to last 3 sts, ssp, p1.

Work 1 row even.

BO rem 5 (5, 6, 6, 6) sts.

FRONT

Work as for back until above armhole shaping and piece measures 19½ (20¾, 21, 22¼, 23)"/50 (53, 53, 57, 58) cm ending with a WS row.

Left Front Neck Shaping

K19 (22, 23, 25, 26) sts, place rem 30 (33, 36, 38, 39) sts on holder.

Dec row 1 (WS): P1, p2tog, work to end of row.

Dec row 2 (RS): Work to last 3 sts, k2tog, k1.

Rep last 2 rows 2 (2, 2, 3, 3) more times. Then rep dec row 1 every RS row 3 (5, 5, 5, 6) times—10 (11, 12, 12, 12) sts rem.

Work even until left front measures 22½ (24, 24½, 26, 27)"/57 (61, 62, 66, 69) cm from beginning, ending with a WS row.

Left Shoulder Shaping

BO 5 (6, 6, 6, 6) at armhole edge. Work 1 row even. BO rem 5 (5, 6, 6, 6) sts.

Right Front Neck Shaping

With RS facing, attach yarn leaving center 11 (11, 13, 13, 13) sts on holder, work to end of row.

Dec row 1 (WS): Work to last 3 sts, ssp, p1.

Dec row 2 (RS): K1, ssk, work to end of row.

Rep last 2 rows 2 (2, 2, 3, 3) more times.

Then rep dec row 2 every RS row 3 (5, 5, 5, 6) times.

Work even until right front measures 22½ (24, 24½, 26, 27)"/57 (61, 62, 66, 64) cm from beginning, ending with a RS row.

Right Shoulder Shaping

BO 5 (6, 6, 6, 6) at armhole edge. Work 1 row even. BO rem 5 (5, 6, 6, 6) sts.

SLEEVES

With 4.0 mm straight needles, CO 42 (42, 44, 50, 50) sts.

Work in garter stitch for 2"/5 cm, ending with a WS row.

Inc row (RS): K10 (10, 12, 13, 13) sts, kfb over next 21 (21, 19, 23, 23) sts, k11 (11, 13, 14, 14) sts—63 (63, 63, 73, 73) sts.

Change to Lace patt and work even until sleeve measures 3¼"/8.2 cm from CO, ending with a WS row.

BO 5 (5, 5, 6, 7) sts at beginning of next 2 rows.

Dec row: K1, k2tog, work to last 3 sts, ssk, k1.

Repeat dec row every row 3 (3, 4, 4, 5) more times—45 (45, 43, 51, 47) sts.

Work even in patt until sleeve measures 6¼ (6¾, 7¼, 7½, 7¾)"/15.8 (17.1, 18, 19, 20) cm from CO, ending with a WS row.

Next row (RS): *K2tog; rep from * to end of row.

Next row (WS): P.

Next row (RS): K2tog, *k2tog, BO 1; rep from * to end.

BO all sts.

FINISHING

Block pieces to finished measurements. Sew shoulder seams.

Neckband

With RS facing and 3.75 mm circular needle, p/u and k3 sts along right back neck, 27 (31, 33, 37, 39) sts from back neck holder, 3 sts along left back neck, 28 (28, 30, 30, 32) sts along left front neck, 11 (11, 13, 13, 13) sts from center front holder, and 28 (28, 30, 30, 32) sts along right front neck—100 (104, 112, 116, 122) sts.

Work in k1, p1 rib for 5 rows.

BO all sts in pattern.

Belt Loops

With crochet hook and leaving a long tail to sew into side seam, chain stitch a 1¾"/4.4 cm-long belt loop for each side seam. Break off yarn, leaving tail to sew into side seam. Sew each end of belt loop securely to each side seam at empire line (where St st and Lace patt meet).

FINISHING

Sew in sleeves, matching shaping.

Sew side and sleeve seams. Weave in all ends. Slide ribbon through belt loops.

SNOW PRINCESS SCHEMATIC

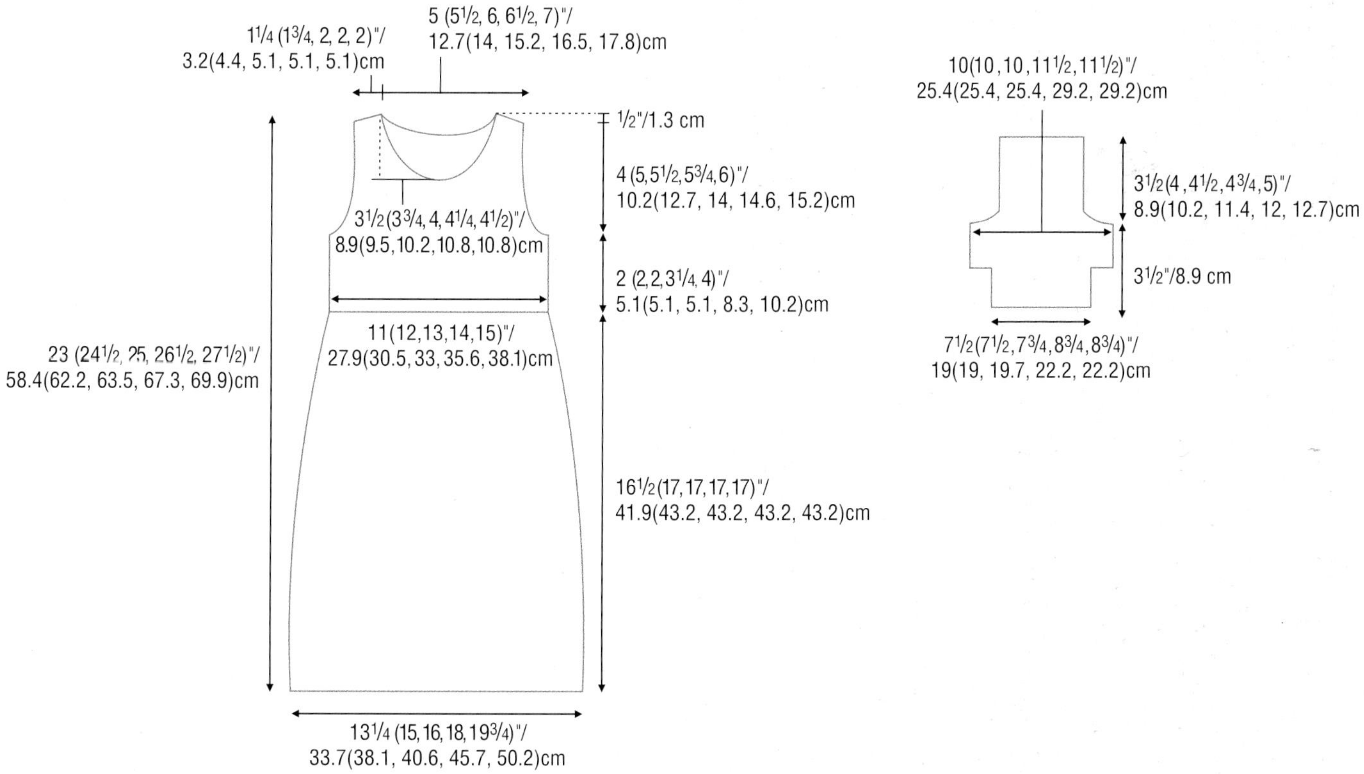
1¼ (1¾, 2, 2, 2)"/
3.2(4.4, 5.1, 5.1, 5.1)cm
5 (5½, 6, 6½, 7)"/
12.7(14, 15.2, 16.5, 17.8)cm
½"/1.3 cm
4 (5,5½,5¾,6)"/
10.2(12.7, 14, 14.6, 15.2)cm
3½(3¾, 4, 4¼, 4½)"/
8.9(9.5,10.2,10.8,10.8)cm
2 (2,2,3¼, 4)"/
5.1(5.1, 5.1, 8.3, 10.2)cm
11(12,13,14,15)"/
27.9(30.5, 33, 35.6, 38.1)cm
23 (24½, 25, 26½, 27½)"/
58.4(62.2, 63.5, 67.3, 69.9)cm
16½(17, 17, 17, 17)"/
41.9(43.2, 43.2, 43.2, 43.2)cm
13¼ (15, 16, 18, 19¾)"/
33.7(38.1, 40.6, 45.7, 50.2)cm
10(10,10,11½,11½)"/
25.4(25.4, 25.4, 29.2, 29.2)cm
3½(4,4½,4¾,5)"/
8.9(10.2, 11.4, 12, 12.7)cm
3½"/8.9 cm
7½(7½,7¾,8¾,8¾)"/
19(19, 19.7, 22.2, 22.2)cm

GOTHIC RAGLAN

CONNIE CHANG CHINCHIO

This raglan boatneck sweater features an unexpected button detail on both sleeves. The allover lace pattern is swirly and organic. Knit in a Japanese wool and silk yarn, this sweater will be a beautiful addition to any fashionista's collection.

SKILL LEVEL

Experienced

SIZES

XS (S, M, L, XL)
34 (38, 42, 46, 50)"/
86 (97, 107, 117, 127) cm
Shown in size XS

FINISHED MEASUREMENTS

Chest and hem circumference: 34¾ (39, 42¾, 47¼, 50½)"/ 88 (99, 109, 120, 128) cm

Finished length: 22¼ (23, 23¾, 24¼, 25)"/57 (58, 60, 62, 64) cm

MATERIALS AND TOOLS

Yarn

1890 (2160, 2160, 2430, 2700) yd/ 1728 (1975, 1975, 2222, 2469) m of fingering weight yarn, 70% wool, 30% silk, in natural

Needles

3.25 mm (size 3 U.S.) circular, 32"/81 cm long
2.75 mm (size 2 U.S.) circular, 32"/81 cm long
or size to obtain gauge

Notions

4 stitch markers
Stitch holders
Tapestry needles
28 (28, 30, 30, 32) buttons
2 hooks and eyes

GAUGE

29 sts and 40 rows = 4"/10.2 cm in Gothic Arches patt on 3.25 mm needles

Always take time to check your gauge.

THIS PROJECT WAS KNIT WITH:

Habu silk wool A-113 (70% wool, 30% silk; 270 yd/50 g): 7 (8, 8, 9, 10) skeins, Kinari (natural)

PATTERN NOTES

One selvedge stitch is worked at each side on the body and sleeves to allow for easier seaming. The selvedge stitch is worked in stockinette stitch, but this is not shown on the schematic.

Work in stockinette stitch on the first 4 stitches and last 4 stitches of the sleeve cap and on the first 4 stitches and last 4 stitches of front and back pieces after armhole shaping begins to facilitate raglan decreases, which are made as follows: k2, ssk, work to last 4 sts, k2tog, k2.

When increasing (decreasing) in Gothic Arches pattern, work increased (decreased) sts in stockinette stitch until there are enough stitches to incorporate the lace stitches (paired decreases and increases) into the pattern.

Increases on the sleeves are worked on the wrong side.

Raglan decreases are worked on the right side and are worked over 4 stockinette stitches.

The basic shape of the raglan is not symmetrical. The front piece has shorter armholes, and the back piece has longer armholes in a shape that conforms to the body's front/back asymmetry.

INSTRUCTIONS

BACK

With 2.75 mm needles, CO 129 (143, 157, 173, 185) sts.

Work 2 rows garter st. Change to 3.25 mm needles.

Next row (RS): K8 (6, 4, 3, 9), work Gothic Arches patt on next 113 (131, 149, 167, 167) sts, k8 (6, 4, 3, 9).

Work as est until piece measures 3"/7.6 cm from CO, ending with a WS row.

Dec row: K1, ssk, work in patt to last 3 sts, k2tog, k1.

Rep dec row every 6 rows 2 more times—123 (137, 151, 167, 179) sts.

Rep dec row every 8 rows 3 times—117 (131, 145, 161, 173) sts.

Work even until piece measures 8¾"/22.2 cm from beg, ending with a WS row.

PATTERN STITCH
GOTHIC ARCHES

Multiple of 18 + 5 sts.

STITCH KEY

Highlighted Repeat

Knit
RS: Knit
WS: Purl

k2tog
RS: Knit two stitches together.

sl1 k2tog, psso
RS: Slip 1, k2tog, pass slipped stitch over, k2tog.

ssk
RS: Slip 1 stitch as if to knit, slip another stitch as if to knit. Insert left-hand needle into the front of these 2 stitches and knit them together.

yo
Yarn Over.

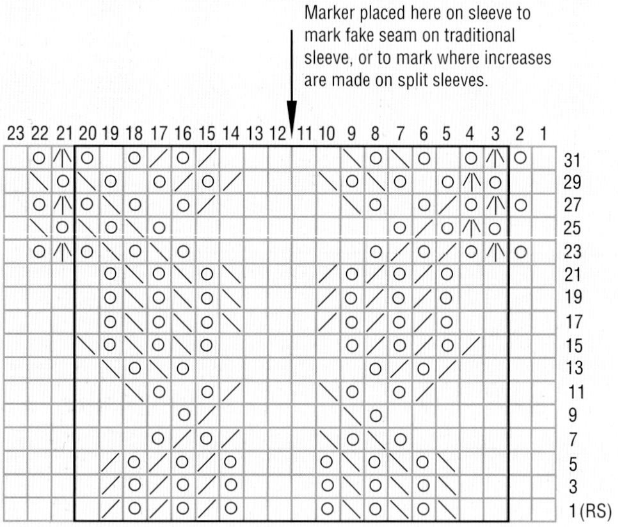
Marker placed here on sleeve to mark fake seam on traditional sleeve, or to mark where increases are made on split sleeves.
23 22 21 20 19 18 17 16 15 14 13 12 11 10 9 8 7 6 5 4 3 2 1
31
29
27
25
23
21
19
17
15
13
11
9
7
5
3
1(RS)

Inc row: K1, m1, work in pattern to last st, m1, k1.

Rep inc row every 8 rows 3 more times—125 (139, 153, 169, 181) sts.

Rep inc row every 10 rows 2 times—129 (143, 157, 173, 185) sts.

Work even until piece measures 13½"/34 cm.

Armhole Shaping

BO 6 (8, 9, 12, 12) sts at beg of next 2 rows.

Working the first 4 sts and last 4 sts in St st throughout during raglan decs (until the last several decs when it becomes necessary to make decs at the edge), work raglan decs as follows.

Dec row: K2, ssk, work to last 4 sts, k2tog, k2.

Rep dec row every RS row 36 (39, 43, 45, 49) times more, ending on a WS row.

BO rem 43 (47, 51, 57, 61) sts.

FRONT

Work as for back until armhole shaping.

Armhole Shaping

BO 6 (8, 9, 12, 12) sts at beg of next 2 rows.

Dec row: K1, ssk, k to last 3 sts, k2tog, k1.

Rep dec row every RS row 26 (29, 33, 35, 39) times more, ending on a WS row—63 (67, 71, 77, 81) sts rem.

Neck Shaping

Next row: K1, ssk, k6, BO 45 (49, 53, 59, 63) sts, k to last 3 sts, k2tog, k1. Attach yarn to the left front neck edge, and work both sides at the same time.

Cont raglan decs and AT THE SAME TIME, dec 1 st at either neck edge every RS row 3 times.

Cont raglan decs until 0 sts rem.

RIGHT SLEEVE

With 2.75 mm needles, CO 61 (63, 81, 95, 99) sts.

Work 2 rows garter st. Change to 3.25 mm needles.

Next row (RS): K1 (2, 2, 0, 2), work in Gothic Arches patt to last 1 (2, 2, 0, 2) sts, k1 (2, 2, 0, 2).

Place markers as follows:

Next row (WS): P30 (31, 40, 47, 49) sts, pm, p31 (32, 41, 48, 50) sts.

Work even as established until piece measures 1¼ (2½, 1¼, 2¾, 1¼)"/3.1 (6.4, 3.1, 6.9, 3.1) cm, ending with a RS row.

Inc row (WS): Work to marker, inc 1, sm, inc 1, work to end.

Rep inc row every 8 (6, 8, 8, 8) rows 19 (23, 19, 17, 19) times more—101 (111, 121, 131, 139) sts.

Work even until piece measures 17"/43 cm, ending with a WS row.

Splitting for Raglan Decs

Next row (RS): Work to marker, remove marker, BO 6 (8, 9, 12, 12) sts, work to end.

Working each side separately, beg raglan decs, keeping first 4 sts on the RS in St st, as follows:

Next row (WS): Work even.

Dec row (RS): K2, ssk, work to end. Rep dec row on RS rows 32 (35, 39, 41, 45) times more, ending with a WS row—11 sts rem.

Next row (RS): BO 4 sts, work to end.

Next row (WS): Work even.

Next row (RS): BO 5 sts, work to end.

Next row (WS): Work even.

Next row (RS): BO 2 sts. Fasten off last st.

Attach yarn to where the split in the sleeve occurs to work the other side of the sleeve, beg with a WS row, as follows.

Next row (WS): BO 6 (8, 9, 12, 12) sts, work to end.

Beg raglan decreases, keeping last 4 sts on the RS in St st.

Dec row (RS): Work to last 4 sts, k2tog, k2.

Rep dec row on RS rows 34 (37, 41, 43, 47) times more, ending with a WS row. Cont raglan decs at the end of RS rows and AT THE SAME TIME BO 3 and BO 5 at the beg of the next 2 RS rows.

LEFT SLEEVE (Shapings Reversed)

Work as for right sleeve until where the sleeve is split for the raglan decs.

Next row row (RS): Work to marker, remove marker, BO 6 (8, 9, 12, 12) sts, work to end.

Working each side separately, beg raglan decs, keeping first 4 sts on the RS in St st, as follows.

Next row (WS): Work even.

Dec row (RS): K2, ssk, work to end.

Rep dec row on RS rows 34 (37, 41, 43, 47) times more, ending with a RS row. Cont raglan decreases at the beg of RS rows and AT THE SAME TIME BO 3 and then BO 5 at the beg of the next 2 WS rows.

Attach yarn where the split in the sleeve occurs to work the other side of the sleeve, beg with a WS row.

Next row (WS): BO 6 (8, 9, 12, 12) sts, work to end.

Beg raglan decreases, keeping last 4 sts on the RS in St st, as follows.

Dec row (RS): Work to last 4 sts, k2tog, k2.

Rep dec row on RS rows 32 (35, 39, 41, 45) times more, ending on a RS row.

Next row (WS): BO 4 sts, work even to end.

Next row (RS): Work even.

Next row (WS): BO 5 sts, work even to end.

Next row (RS): Work even.

Next row (WS): BO 2 sts.

FINISHING

Sew in sleeves at raglan edges. Sew side seams.

Sleeves

With 2.75 mm needles and RS facing, p/u 176 (181, 187, 190, 196) sts along left side edge of sleeve.

Work 3 rows garter st.

BO all sts knitwise.

With 2.75 mm needles and RS facing, p/u 149 (151, 154, 156, 159) sts along right side edge of sleeve.

Work 1 row garter st.

Next row: K10 (12, 9, 11, 8), *yo, k2tog, k10; rep from * to last 10 (13, 10, 11, 8) sts, yo, k2tog, k to end.

Work 1 row garter st.

BO all sts knitwise.

Attach buttons to left side to match buttonholes on right side. Button up sleeves to prepare for applying neck border.

Neck Border

With 2.75 mm needles and with RS facing, p/u 13 sts along the top half of the left sleeve attached to the front piece, 57 (60, 65, 71, 75) sts along front neck, 13 sts along the top half of the right sleeve attached to the front piece—83 (86, 91, 97, 101) sts total.

Work 2 rows in garter st. BO all sts.

With 2.75 mm needles and with RS facing, p/u 9 sts along the top half of the right sleeve attached to the back piece, 43 (47, 51, 57, 61) sts along back neck, and 9 sts along the top half of the right sleeve attached to the back piece—61 (65, 69, 75, 79) total.

Work 2 rows in garter st. BO all sts.

Sew hook and eye at top inside edges of both sleeves.

GOTHIC RAGLAN SCHEMATIC

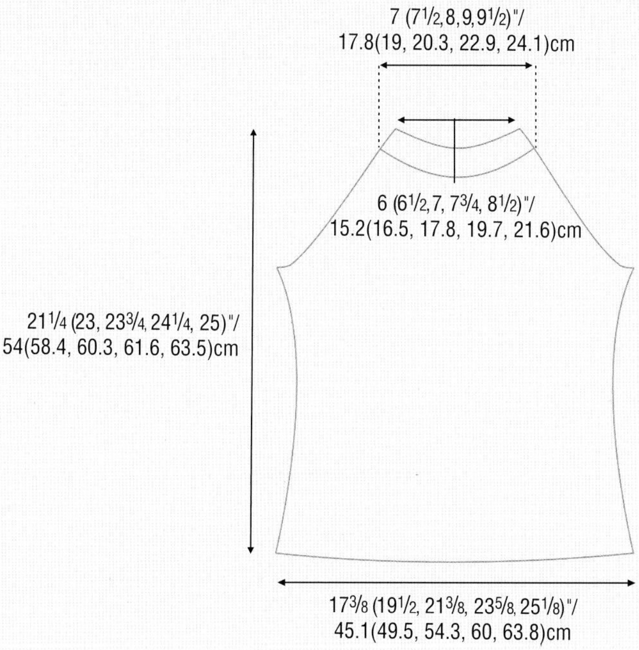
7 (7 1/2, 8, 9, 9 1/2)"/
17.8(19, 20.3, 22.9, 24.1)cm
7 1/2 (8 1/4, 9, 9 1/2, 10 1/4)"/
19(21, 22.9, 24.1, 26)cm
6 (6 1/2, 7, 7 3/4, 8 1/2)"/
15.2(16.5, 17.8, 19.7, 21.6)cm
21 1/4 (23, 23 3/4, 24 1/4, 25)"/
54(58.4, 60.3, 61.6, 63.5)cm
13 1/2"/34.3 cm
17 3/8 (19 1/2, 21 3/8, 23 5/8, 25 1/8)"/
45.1(49.5, 54.3, 60, 63.8)cm

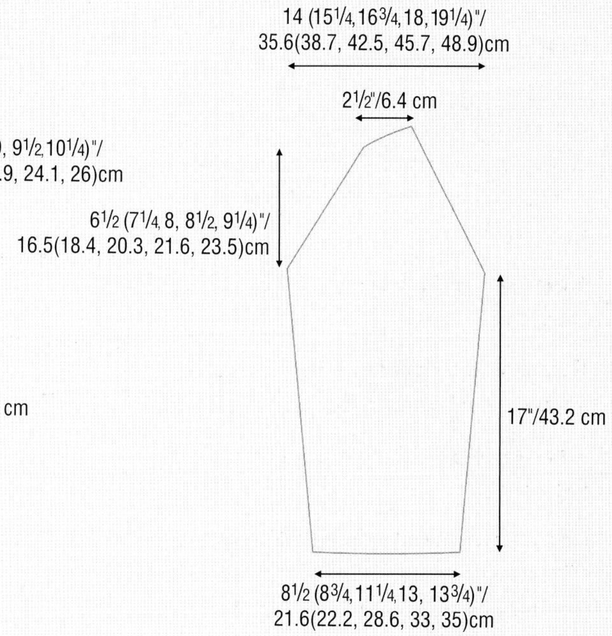
14 (15 1/4, 16 3/4, 18, 19 1/4)"/
35.6(38.7, 42.5, 45.7, 48.9)cm
2 1/2"/6.4 cm
6 1/2 (7 1/4, 8, 8 1/2, 9 1/4)"/
16.5(18.4, 20.3, 21.6, 23.5)cm
17"/43.2 cm
8 1/2 (8 3/4, 11 1/4, 13, 13 3/4)"/
21.6(22.2, 28.6, 33, 35)cm

CHAPTER 4

Arctic Cables

CABLED BABY SET

LEAH BEAR

Classic cables are revisited with this chic baby set. The cables ascend from largest to smallest on the hat and descend from smallest to largest on the booties. The booties are worked with the cable stitches reversed on the cuffs so they match perfectly when rolled down. The stretch of the cable rib makes these knits perfect for babies' growth spurts. The merino/alpaca blend is soft enough for a baby's skin and luxe enough to make a perfect shower gift. One skein will make a hat and booties in the largest size.

SKILL LEVEL

Intermediate/Experienced

SIZES

6 (12, 18) months
Shown in size 18 months

FINISHED MEASUREMENTS

Head circumference: 12 (14, 16)"/31 (36, 41) cm
Foot Length: 2½ (3½, 4½)"/ 6.4 (8.9, 11.4) cm

MATERIALS AND TOOLS

Yarn

350 yd/320 m of sport weight yarn, 60% merino wool, 40% alpaca, in eggshell

Needles

3.25 mm (size 3 U.S.) dpns
or size to obtain gauge

Notions

Cable needle or extra double pointed needle
Tapestry needle
Stitch holder

GAUGE

36 sts and 36 rnds = 4"/10.2 cm in Cable Stitch knit in the round

Always take time to check your gauge.

THIS PROJECT WAS KNIT WITH:

Pear Tree Shades of Alpaca 4-ply Sport (60% Australian merino, 40% alpaca, 350 yd/ 100 g); 1 skein, Eggshell

2

PATTERN NOTES

For the booties, the cable pattern is worked inside out on the first 1 (1½, 2)"/2.5 (3.8, 5) cm of the cuff so it is visible when the cuff is folded down.

PATTERN STITCHES

3-STITCH RIGHT CABLE (3-ST RC)

Slip 2 stitches to cable needle and hold in back of work, k1, k2 from cable needle.

3-STITCH PURLED TWIST (3-ST RPC)

Slip next stitch purlwise and hold in back of work, p2, then p1 from cable needle.

INSTRUCTIONS

CABLED HAT

With the long-tail cast on, CO 105 (125, 145) sts and distribute on 3 needles as follows.

Size 6 months: 35 sts on each needle.

Size 12 months: 40 sts on needles 1 and 2 and 45 sts on needle 3.

Size 18 months: 50 sts on needles 1 and 2 and 45 sts on needle 3.

Pm and join to knit in the rnd, being careful not to twist sts.

Rnds 1–6: *K3, p2, rep from * to end.

Rnd 7: *3-St RC, p2, rep from * to end.

Rnds 8–12: *K3, p2, rep from * to end.

Rnd 13: *3-St RC, p2, rep from * to end.

Rnds 14–17: *K3, p2, rep from * to end.

Rnd 18: *3-St RC, p2, rep from * to end.

Rnds 19–21: *K3, p2, rep from * to end.

Rnd 22: *3-St RC, p2, rep from * to end.

Rnds 23–24: *K3, p2, rep from * to end.

Rnd 25: *3-St RC, p2, rep from * to end.

Rep rnds 23–25 until piece measures 3 (3½, 4)"/7.6 (8.9, 10.2) cm or desired length, ending with a cable rnd.

Beg Dec Rnds

Rnd 1: *K8, p2tog, repeat from * to end—95 (113, 131) sts rem.

Rnd 2: *K3, p2, k3, p1, rep from * to end.

Rnd 3: *3-St RC, p2, k2, p2tog, rep from * to end—85 (101, 117) sts rem.

Rnd 4: *K3, p2, k2, p1, rep from * to end.

Rnd 5: *K3, p2, k1, p2tog, rep from * to end—75 (89, 103) sts rem.

Rnd 6: *3-St RC, p2, p2tog, rep from * to end—65 (77, 89) sts rem.

Rnd 7: *K3, p1, p2tog, rep from * to end—55 (65, 75) sts rem.

Rnd 8: *K3, p2tog, rep from * to end—44 (52, 60) sts rem.

Rnd 9: *K2, k2tog, rep from * to end.

Rep rnd 9 until 12 (14, 11) sts rem.

K2tog to end until 3 (3, 3) sts rem.

FINISHING

Break yarn, pull through remaining 3 sts, and tighten to gather. Weave in ends. Block if desired.

CABLED BOOTIES

CO 35 (40, 45) sts, distribute sts evenly on 3 needles, pm, and join to k in the rnd, being careful not to twist sts.

Rnds 1– 2: *P3, k2, rep from * to end.

Rnd 3: *3-st RPC, p2, rep from * to end.

Repeat rnds 1–3 until piece measures 1 (1½, 2)"/2.5 (3.8, 5) cm from CO, ending with rnd 3.

Rnds 4–5: *K3, p2, rep from * to end.

Rnd 6: *3-St RC, p2, rep from * to end.

Repeat rnds 4–6 until piece measures 2½ (3, 3½)"/6.4 (7.6, 8.9) cm from CO (without cuff rolled), ending with rnd 6.

Instep

Rnd 7: *K3, p2 on 23 sts, then remove these sts to a st holder.

Rem 12 (17, 22) sts will be worked back and forth for the instep as follows.

Note: *Sl sts at beg of each rnd to create a chain edge.*

Size 6 months: Work rows 1–13.

Size 12 months: Work rows 1–23.

Size 18 months: Work rows 1–33.

Row 1: Sl1 pwise, p1, *k3, p2, rep from * to end.

Row 2: Sl1 kwise, k1, *p3, k2, rep from * to end.

Row 3: Sl1 pwise, p1, *3-St RC, p2, rep from * to end.

Row 4: Sl1 kwise, k1, *p3, k2, rep from * to end.

Row 5: Sl1 pwise, p1, *k3, p2, rep from * to end.

Row 6: Sl1 kwise, k1, *p3, k2, rep from * to end.

Row 7: Sl1 pwise, p1, *3-St RC, p2, rep from * to end.

Row 8: Sl1 kwise, k1, *p3, k2, rep from * to end.

Row 9: Sl1 pwise, p1, *k3, p2, rep from * to end.

Row 10: Sl1 kwise, k1, *p3, k2, rep from * to end.

Row 11: Sl1 pwise, p1, *k3, p2, rep from * to end.

Row 12: Sl1 kwise, k1, *p3, k2, rep from * to end.

Row 13: Sl1 pwise, p1, *3-St RC, p2, rep from * to end.

Row 14: Sl1 kwise, k1, *p3, k2, rep from * to end.

Row 15: Sl1 pwise, p1, *k3, p2, rep from * to end.

Row 16: Sl1 kwise, k1, *p3, k2, rep from * to end.

Row 17: Sl1 pwise, p1, *k3, p2, rep from * to end.

Row 18: Sl1 kwise, k1, *p3, k2, rep from * to end.

Row 19: Sl1 pwise, p1, *3-St RC, p2, rep from * to end.

Row 20: Sl1 kwise, k1, *p3, k2, rep from * to end.

Row 21: Sl1 pwise, p1, *k3, p2, rep from * to end.

Row 22: Sl1 kwise, k1, *p3, k2, rep from * to end.

Row 23: Sl1 pwise, p1, *k3, p2, rep from * to end.

Row 24: Sl1 kwise, k1, *p3, k2, rep from * to end.

Row 25: Sl1 pwise, p1, *3-St RC, p2, rep from * to end.

Row 26: Sl1 kwise, k1, *p3, k2, rep from * to end.

Row 27: Sl1 pwise, p1, *k3, p2, rep from * to end.

Row 28: Sl1 kwise, k1, *p3, k2, rep from * to end.

Row 29: Sl1 pwise, p1, *k3, p2, rep from * to end.

Row 30: Sl1 kwise, k1, *p3, k2, rep from * to end.

Row 31: Sl1 pwise, p1, *3-St RC, p2, rep from * to end.

Row 32: Sl1 kwise, k1, *p3, k2, rep from * to end.

Row 33: Sl1 pwise, p1, *k3, p2, rep from * to end.

Begin Side

With right side of work facing and with working yarn at the left top of the instep, p/u and k6 (11, 16) sts along the left side of the instep; k the 23 sts from the holder; p/u and k6 (11, 16) sts from the right side of the instep; k12 (17, 22) sts across the instep.

Work 6 (8, 10) rounds in St st.

Begin Sole

Distribute sts on 4 dpns as follows.

Size 6 months: 8 sts on needle 1, 16 sts on needle 2, 8 sts on needle 3 and 15 sts on needle 4.

Size 12 months: 10 sts on needle 1, 21 sts on needle 2, 10 sts on needle 3 and 21 sts on needle 4.

Size 18 months:12 sts on needle 1, 27 sts on needle 2, 12 sts on needle 3 and 26 sts on needle 4.

Sole Dec Rnd (for sizes 6 months and 18 months only): K all sts on needle 1, ssk, k to end of needle 2, k all sts on needles 3 and 4—46 (66, 76) sts rem.

Beg Sole Shaping

Rnd 1: Ssk, k4 (6, 8), k2tog, k15 (21, 26), ssk, k4 (6,8), k2tog, k15 (21, 26).

Rnd 2: Ssk, k2 (4, 6), k2tog, k15 (21, 26), ssk, k2 (4,6), k2tog, k15 (21, 26).

Rnd 3: Ssk, k0 (2, 4), k2tog, k15 (21, 26), ssk, k0 (2, 4), k2tog, k15 (21, 26).

Size 12 months and 18 months only

Rnd 4: Ssk, k0 (2), k2tog, k21 (26), ssk, k0 (2), k2tog, k21 (26).

Size 18 months only

Rnd 5: Ssk, k2tog, k26, ssk, k2tog, k26.

FINISHING

Work 1 rnd as follows: K2tog, k15 (21, 26), k2tog, k15 (21, 26).

Move sts from needle 1 to needle 2 and from needle 3 to needle 4—16 (22, 27) sts on needles 2 and 4.

Use the Kitchener stitch to graft these 32 (44, 54) sts together.

Weave in ends. Block grafted area.

CAMERON SKI CAP AND SCARF SET

ANDREA TUNG

Cozy knits and an old English village backdrop is my idea of a perfect holiday. Don't forget to pack accessories such as this cap and scarf set, which feature cable detailing. Both are knit in the round with two or three strands held together.

SKILL LEVEL

Intermediate

SIZES

Women's, one size

FINISHED MEASUREMENTS

Head circumference: 21"/53 cm
Cap length: 8½"/22 cm
Scarf length: 73"/185 cm
Scarf width: 2"/5 cm

MATERIALS AND TOOLS

Yarn

435 yd/398 m of DK weight yarn, 100% baby alpaca, in natural for cap 580 yd/530 m of DK weight yarn, 100% baby alpaca, in natural for scarf

Needles

4.5 mm (size 7 U.S.) dpns
5.5 mm (size 9 U.S.) 16"/41 cm long, circular
5.5 mm (size 9 U.S.) dpns
or size to obtain gauge

Notions

Cable needle
Stitch markers
Tapestry needle
Crochet hook
Scissors

GAUGE

19 sts and 24 rows = 4"/10.2 cm on 4.5 mm needles
16 sts and 24 rows= 4"/10.2 cm on 5.5 mm needles

Always take time to check your gauge.

THIS PROJECT WAS KNIT WITH:

Fable Handknit Pure Baby Alpaca (100% baby alpaca; 145 yd/50 g): 3 skeins for cap, 4 skeins for scarf, Natural (06)

3

INSTRUCTIONS

CAP

With 5.5 mm circular needles and 3 strands of yarn held together, CO 80 sts. Pm and join rnd, being careful not to twist sts.

Work 4 rows in k1, p1 ribbing.

Work in cable patt as follows.

Rnds 1–9: *K10, p10, rep from * to end.

Rnd 10: *Sl5 sts onto cn and hold in front of work, k5, k5 from cn, p10, rep from * to end.

Rnds 11–24: *K10, p10, rep from * to end.

Rnd 25: *Sl5 sts onto cn and hold in front of work, k5, k5 from cn, p10, rep from * to end.

Beg dec rnds, switching to dpns when necessary, as follows.

Rnd 1: *K10, p2tog tbl, p6, p2tog, rep from * to end.

Rnd 2: *K10, p8, rep from * to end.

Rnd 3: *K10, p2tog tbl, p4, p2tog, rep from * to end.

Rnd 4: *K10, p6, rep from * to end.

Rnd 5: *K10, p2tog tbl, p2, p2tog, rep from * to end.

Rnd 6: *K10, p4, rep from * to end.

Rnd 7: *K10, p2tog tbl, p2tog, rep from * to end.

Rnd 8: *K10, p2, rep from * to end.

Rnd 9: *K2tog 5 times, p2tog, rep from * to end.

Rnd 10: *K2tog, rep from * to end (12 sts rem).

Break yarn, leaving a 10"/25.4 cm tail. Draw tail through rem sts twice, pulling tightly to gather, and knot. Pull end to inside and weave in ends.

SCARF

With 4.5 mm dpns and 2 strands of yarn held together, CO 32 sts and distribute evenly on 3 needles. Pm and join rnd, being careful not to twist sts.

Work 15 rnds in St st.

Beg cable patt as follows.

Rnd 1: Sl8 sts onto cn and hold in front of work, k8, k8 from cn, k16.

Rnds 2–9: Knit.

Rnd 10: K16, sl8 sts onto cn and hold in front of work, k8 from cn.

Rnds 11–18: Knit.

Rep cable patt 29 times or to desired length.

Work 7 rnds in St st. BO all sts.

FINISHING

Cut 48 strands of yarn, 18"/146 cm long. For each fringe, fold 3 strands of yarn together and fold in half to create a loop. Using a crochet hook, pull loop through both layers of scarf edge, and then pull ends of yarn through loop. Make 8 to 10 fringe on each edge. Trim ends even.

BOY'S CABLED RAGLAN SWEATER

ALLISON BLEVINS

Subtle stripes and ribbed edges add a collegiate feel to this cute raglan. The sweater incorporates slightly different shades of white, adding aesthetic interest and crisp lines. The tiny cables in the raglan line and along the sides add texture and shaping to this darling piece.

SKILL LEVEL

Intermediate

SIZES

2 (4, 6, 8, 12)
Shown in size 2

FINISHED MEASUREMENTS

Chest and hem circumference: 21 (23, 25, 27, 30)"/53 (58, 64, 69, 76) cm
Length: 13½ (14½, 16½, 18½, 20½)"/ 34 (37, 42, 47, 52) cm
Sleeve length: 7½ (9½, 10½, 12, 14½)"/19 (24, 27, 31, 37) cm

MATERIALS AND TOOLS

Yarn

Color A: 175 (350, 525, 700, 875) yd/ 160 (320, 480, 640, 800) m of DK weight yarn, 100% superwash merino wool, in white
Color B: 175 (350, 525, 700, 875) yd/ 160 (320, 480, 640, 800) m of DK weight yarn, 100% superwash merino wool, in cream

Needles

4.0 mm (size 6 U.S.) circular, 16"/41 cm and 24"/61 cm long
or size to obtain gauge

Notions

Stitch markers
Row counter
Tapestry needle
Cable needle

GAUGE

20 sts and 24 rows = 4"/ 10.2 cm in St st

Always take time to check your gauge.

THIS PROJECT WAS KNIT WITH:

Yarn A: Louet Gems Worsted Weight (100% Superwash Merino Wool; 175 yd/100 g): 1 (2, 3, 4, 5) skeins White (70)

Yarn B: Louet Gems Worsted Weight (100% Superwash Merino Wool; 175 yd/100 g): 1 (2, 3, 4, 5) skeins Cream (30)

PATTERN NOTES

Sweater is worked from the top down.

Slip all markers unless otherwise noted. Slip all stitches purlwise unless otherwise noted.

Stripes are 8 rows high alternating Yarn B and Yarn A. Follow this pattern for body and sleeve stripes.

PATTERN STITCHES

CABLE 4

Sl2 sts to cn and hold needle in front of work, k2 sts, k2 sts from cn.

CABLE 8

Sl4 sts to cn and hold in front of work, k4 sts, k4 sts from cn.

INSTRUCTIONS

NECK

With 16"/41 cm circular needle, CO 50 (50, 58, 58, 64) sts.

Raglan Shaping

Row 1: P2, pm, p4, pm, p8 (8, 10, 10, 12), pm, p4, pm, p14 (14, 18, 18, 20), pm, p4, pm p8 (8, 10, 10, 12), pm, p4, pm, p2.

Row 2: **Kfb, k to within 1 st of next m, kfb, sm, k4, sm,** rep between ** to last m, kfb, k to last st, kfb.

Row 3: P.

Row 4: **Kfb, k to within 1 st of next m, kfb, sm, cable 4, sm,** rep between * to last m, kfb, k to last st, kfb.

Row 5: P.

Rep rows 2–5 until there are 8 (8, 10, 12, 14) sts before 1st m on RS, ending with a k row.

CO 4 (4, 6, 4, 4) sts, pm, and join to work in the rnd—84 (84, 104, 112, 128) sts.

Note: *Change colors for stripes at the first raglan m of the rnd.*

Cont to work cables as established and work as follows.

Rnd 1: K.

Rnd 2 (Inc): **K to within 1 st of next m, kfb, sm, k4, sm,** rep between ** to last m, kfb, k to end of rnd.

Repeat rnds 1 and 2, cont to cable every four rnds as est until there are 40 (44, 48, 52, 60) sts between sleeve ms. Change to 24"/61 cm circular needle when needed.

Removing Sleeve Sts

Next rnd: K to 2nd m, **remove m, place 40 (44, 48, 52, 60) sts on waste yarn (for sleeve), remove next m, ktbl,** k to next set of ms, rep between ** once, k to end of rnd.

Note: *5 markers rem—1 to mark beg of round, two on each side mark cables. There are 8 sts between each set of cable markers.*

Rnds 1–5: K even.

Rnd 6 (Cable): K to first set of ms, **sm, cable 8, sm,** k to next set of ms, rep between **, k to end of rnd.

Rnds 7–12: K even.

Repeat rnds 1–12 until piece measures 12 (13, 15, 17, 19)" from top of shoulder (or 1½" less than desired length).

Work in k1, p1 rib for 1½"/3.8 cm.

BO in patt.

SLEEVES

Transfer 40 (44, 48, 52, 60) sleeve sts from waste yarn to dpns. Attach yarn to right of underarm and p/u 4 sts evenly across underarm gap, pm after 2 sts (beg of rnd). K to end of rnd.

K 2 rounds even.

Rnd 1 (Dec): K1, ssk, k to last 3 sts, k2tog, k1.

Rnds 2–6: K even.

Rep rnds 1–6 4 (5, 6, 6, 8) times—32 (34, 36, 40, 44) sts rem.

Work even until sleeve measures 7 (9, 10, 11, 13½)"/17.8(22.9, 25.4, 27.9, 34.3) cm from underarm.

Work in k1, p1 rib for 4 (4, 4, 6, 6) rnds. BO loosely in patt.

NECKBAND

P/u 68 (72, 88, 96, 112) sts evenly spaced around neckline—12 (12, 15, 16, 19) sts for each sleeve cap and 22 (24, 29, 32, 37) sts each for front and back.

Pm and join to work in the rnd.

Work in k1, p1 rib for 4 (4, 4, 6, 6) rnds. BO loosely in patt.

FINISHING

Weave in ends. Block as needed.

BOY'S CABLED RAGLAN SWEATER SCHEMATIC

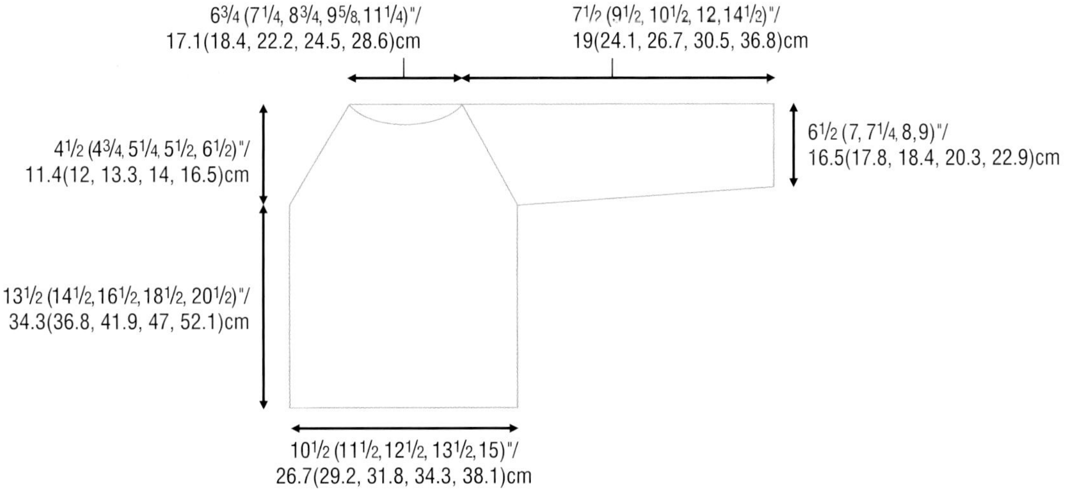
6¾ (7¼, 8¾, 9⅝, 11¼)"/
17.1(18.4, 22.2, 24.5, 28.6)cm
7½ (9½, 10½, 12, 14½)"/
19(24.1, 26.7, 30.5, 36.8)cm
4½ (4¾, 5¼, 5½, 6½)"/
11.4(12, 13.3, 14, 16.5)cm
6½ (7, 7¼, 8, 9)"/
16.5(17.8, 18.4, 20.3, 22.9)cm
13½ (14½, 16½, 18½, 20½)"/
34.3(36.8, 41.9, 47, 52.1)cm
10½ (11½, 12½, 13½, 15)"/
26.7(29.2, 31.8, 34.3, 38.1)cm

GIRL'S CABLED VICTORIAN DRESS

ALLISON BLEVINS

This surprisingly quick knit dress will bring pizazz to your favorite spunky girl's wardrobe. The detailed edging adds the perfect amount of texture without overpowering the drape of stockinette. A delicate picot hem frames the dainty skirt.

SKILL LEVEL

Intermediate

SIZES

2 (4, 6, 8, 12)
Shown in size 4

FINISHED MEASUREMENTS

Chest: 21 (23, 25, 27, 30)"/ 53 (58, 64, 69, 76) cm

Length: 18 (22, 23½, 26½, 29½)"/46 (55, 60, 67, 75) cm

Sleeves: 8½ (10½, 11½, 12½, 15)"/22 (27, 29, 32, 38) cm

MATERIALS AND TOOLS

Yarn

700 (700, 875, 875, 875) yd/ 640 (640, 800, 800, 800) m of light worsted weight yarn, 100% superwash merino wool, in cream

Needles

4.0 mm (size 6 U.S.) circular, 16"/41 cm and 24"/61 cm long
4.0 mm (size 6 U.S.) dpns
or size to obtain gauge

Notions

Stitch markers
Row counter
Tapestry needle
Cable needle

GAUGE

20 sts and 24 rnds = 4"/ 10.2 cmin St st

Always take time to check your gauge.

THIS PROJECT WAS KNIT WITH:

Louet Gems Worsted Weight (100% Superwash Merino Wool; 175 yd/100 g): 4 (4, 5, 5, 5) skeins, Cream (30)

PATTERN NOTES

Dress is worked from the top down. Pass all markers unless otherwise noted.

Slip all stitches purlwise unless otherwise noted.

PATTERN STITCHES

Cable 3: Sl2 sts to cn and hold in front of work, k1 st, k2 sts from cn.

Cable 4: Sl2 sts to cn and hold in front of work, k2 sts, k2 sts from cn.

Cable 8: Sl4 sts to cn and hold in front of work, k4 sts, k4 sts from cn.

CABLE RIB

Multiple of 4 sts.

Rnd 1: K3, p1.

Rnd 2: Cable 3, p1.

Repeat rnds 1 and 2.

INSTRUCTIONS

NECKLINE

With 16"/41 cm circular needles, CO 50 (50, 58, 58, 64) sts.

Raglan Shaping

Work back and forth as for flat knitting.

Row 1: P2, pm, p4, pm, p8 (8, 10, 10, 12), pm, p4, pm, p14 (14, 18, 18, 20), pm, p4, pm, p8 (8, 10, 10, 12), pm, p4, pm, p2.

Row 2: **Kfb, k to within 1 st of next marker, kfb, sm, k4, pm,** repeat between ** to last marker, kfb, k to last st, kfb.

Row 3: P.

Row 4: **Kfb, k to within 1 st of next marker, kfb, sm, cable 4, pm** rep between ** to last marker, kfb, k to last st, kfb.

Row 5: P.

Rep rows 2–5 until there are 8 (8, 10, 12, 14) sts before the 1st marker on RS, ending with a k row—80 (80, 98, 108, 120) sts.

CO 4 (4, 6, 4, 4) sts, pm, join to work in the rnd—84 (84, 104, 112, 128) sts.

Cont cable patt, work as follows.

Next rnd: K.

Next rnd (inc): **K to within 1 st of next m, kfb, sm, k4, sm,** repeat between ** to last m, kfb, k to end of rnd.

Rep last 2 rnds until there are 40 (44, 48, 52, 60) sts between sleeve ms.

Change to 24"/61 cm circular needles when there are enough sts.

Removing Sleeve Sts

Next rnd: K to 2nd m, **remove m, place next 40 (44, 48, 52, 60) sts (for sleeve) on waste yarn, remove next m, ktbl of next st,** k to next set of sleeve stitches (6th m), rep between ** once, k to end of rnd. 5 ms rem—1 marks beg of rnd, 2 on each side mark cables. There are 8 sts between each set of cable markers.

Rnd 1: K.

Rnd 2 (inc): K to 1 st before first cable m, **m1, k1, sm, k8, sm, k1, m1,** knit to 1st before next cable m, rep between **, k to end of rnd.

Rnds 3–5: K even.

Rnd 6 (Cable): K to 1st cable m, **sm, cable 8, sm,** k to next cable m, repeat between **, k to end of rnd.

Rnds 7–9: K even.

Rnd 10: Repeat rnd 2.

Cont to work in St st, working an inc every 8 rnds and a cable every 12 rnds until piece measures 17 (21, 23½, 26½, 29½)"/43 (53, 60, 67, 75) cm from top of shoulder or 1"/12.5 cm less than desired length.

Picot Hem

Rnds 1–6: K even.

Rnd 7: *K2tog, yo* rep to end.

Rnds 8–13: K6 even.

Fold hem to inside along picot rnd and sew stitches securely on WS.

SLEEVES (Make 2)

Transfer 40 (44, 48, 52, 60) sleeve sts from waste yarn to dpns or to short circular needle. Attach yarn to right of underarm and p/u 6 sts evenly across underarm gap, pm after 3 sts at beg of rnd.

Next rnd: K even.

Creating the Pouf

Next rnd: K14 (16, 18, 20, 24), **pm, ssk, k3,** rep between ** 3 times, k to end of rnd.

Next rnd: K to 1st m, **sm, ssk, k2,** rep between ** 3 times, k to end of rnd.

Next rnd: K to 1st m, **remove m, ssk, k1,** rep between ** 3 times, k to end of rnd.

Next 5 rnds: K even.

Next rnd (dec): K1, ssk, k to last 3 sts, k2tog, k1.

Cont k even for 5 rounds and dec every 6 rnds until 34 (34, 36, 40, 44) sts rem.

Work even until sleeve measures 5 (7, 7½, 8, 10)"/12.7 (17.8, 19, 20.3, 25.4) cm from underarm, or 3½ (3½, 4, 4½, 5)"/8.6 (8.9, 10.2, 11.4, 12.7) cm less than desired length.

Size 2 (4) only:

Inc 2 sts as follows: k1, m1, k to last stitch, m1, k1.

All Sizes:

Work in cable rib for 3½ (3½, 4, 4½, 5)"/8.9 (8.9, 10.2, 11.4, 12.7) cm.

BO loosely.

Rep for other sleeve.

NECK

P/u 68 (72, 88, 96, 112) sts evenly spaced around neck—12 (12, 15, 16, 19) sts for each sleeve cap and 22 (24, 29, 32, 37) sts each for front and back. Pm and join to work in the rnd. Work

1"/2.5 cm in cable rib.

BO very loosely in patt.

FINISHING

Weave in all ends. Block as needed.

GIRL'S CABLED VICTORIAN DRESS SCHEMATIC

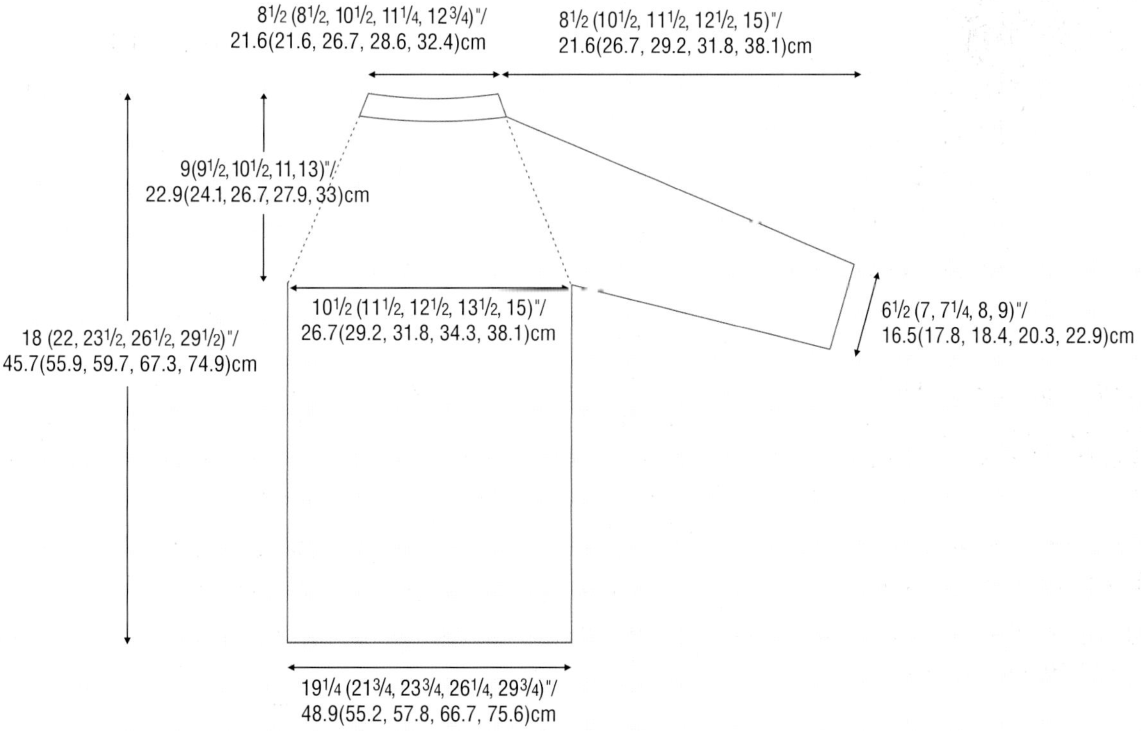
8½ (8½, 10½, 11¼, 12¾)"/
21.6(21.6, 26.7, 28.6, 32.4)cm
8½ (10½, 11½, 12½, 15)"/
21.6(26.7, 29.2, 31.8, 38.1)cm
9(9½, 10½, 11, 13)"/
22.9(24.1, 26.7, 27.9, 33)cm
10½ (11½, 12½, 13½, 15)"/
26.7(29.2, 31.8, 34.3, 38.1)cm
18 (22, 23½, 26½, 29½)"/
45.7(55.9, 59.7, 67.3, 74.9)cm
6½ (7, 7¼, 8, 9)"/
16.5(17.8, 18.4, 20.3, 22.9)cm
19¼ (21¾, 23¾, 26¼, 29¾)"/
48.9(55.2, 57.8, 66.7, 75.6)cm

ORCHID SWEATER

ILLANNA WEINER

The luxurious Orchid Sweater will transform you into an elegant flower. This body-hugging piece accentuates the feminine curves of all body types. Orchid is full-fashioned with strategically placed slipped stitches and fun-to-knit rib and cable patterns that will draw the fabric to your body. Fashion meets function with a construction that is as unique as the sweater's floral namesake.

SKILL LEVEL

Intermediate

SIZES

XS (S, M, L, XL, 2XL, 3XL)
30 (32, 34, 36, 38, 40, 42)"/
76 (81, 86, 91, 97, 102, 107) cm
Shown in size XS

FINISHED MEASUREMENTS

Chest: 30 (32, 34, 36, 38, 40, 42)"/
76 (81, 86, 91, 97, 102, 107) cm

MATERIALS AND TOOLS

Yarn

871 (938, 1072, 1206, 1273, 1407, 1474) yd/796 (858, 980, 1103, 1164, 1287, 1348) m of DK weight yarn, 50% extrafine merino, 25% silk, 25% cashmere, in white

Needles

4.0 mm (size 6 U.S.) circular, 12"/31 cm and 24–32"/61-81 cm long
4.0 mm (size 6 U.S.) dpns
or size to obtain gauge

Notions

Tapestry needle
Removable stitch markers or scrap yarn
4 stitch holders or scrap yarn

GAUGE

20 sts and 28 rows = 4"/10.2 cm in St st
21 sts and 28 rows = 4"/10.2 cm in k2, p1 rib, slightly stretchod
24 sts and 28 rows = 4"/10.2 cm in Cable patt, slightly stretched

Always take time to check your gauge.

THIS PROJECT WAS KNIT WITH:

Laines Du Nord "Cash-Silk"
(50% extrafine merino, 25% silk, 25% cashmere; 67 yd/25 g):
13 (14, 16, 18, 19, 21, 22) balls, white (1)

PATTERN NOTES

Orchid is a seamless sweater, with the body and sleeves knit in the round from the bottom up. The underarm stitches are held on stitch holders or waste yarn until they are woven together at the end.

The front of the sweater contains most of the shaping. Below the bust line, the cabled stitch pattern pulls in at the waist and allows for ease at the hips. Above the bust line, stockinette stitch provides a backdrop for a centered slip stitch pattern that shapes the bust. The back of the sweater features an allover cable pattern, producing a stretchy fabric that fits all body types beautifully.

Align the yoke decreases by working to 1 stitch before the marked stitch and then working the double decrease.

SPECIAL ABBREVIATIONS

RT (Right Twist): Knit the next 2 stitches together, but do not pull off needle. Knit into first stitch on the left hand needle. Drop both sts off left-hand needle.

Sl2, k1, p2sso: Slip 2 stitches together knitwise with yarn in back, knit 1, pass 2 slipped stiched over.

INSTRUCTIONS

BODY

Using longer circular needle, CO 150 (159, 168, 180, 189, 201, 210) sts. Pm and join to work in the rnd, being careful not to twist sts.

Work Tiny Cables patt in the rnd for 11½ (12, 12½, 13, 13½, 14, 14½)"/29 (31, 32, 33, 34, 36, 37) cm ending with row 4 of the cable pattern repeat.

Work Tiny Cables patt on next 75 (79, 84, 90, 96, 99, 105) sts (for Back), pm, work St st on next 74 (79, 83, 89, 92, 101, 104) sts (for Front), pm, p1, remove original m.

Cont to work as est until piece measures 13 (13½, 14, 15, 15½, 16½, 17)"/33 (34, 36, 38, 39, 42, 43) cm from CO edge.

PATTERN STITCHES

FRONT ORCHID PATTERN

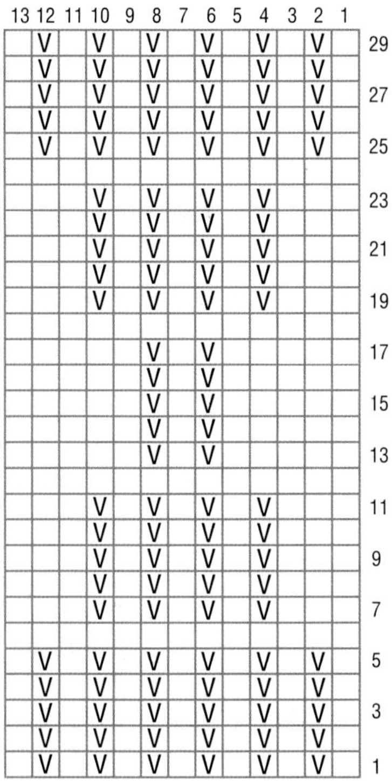

STITCH KEY

☐ Knit

V Slip 1 stitch as if to purl, holding yarn at back.

Tiny Cables

Rows 1–3: *P1, k2

Row 4: *P1, RT

Begin working bust shaping as follows:

Work Tiny Cables patt over back sts, k30 (33, 35, 38, 39, 44, 45) sts, sm, work 13 sts following Orchid patt chart, sm, k31 (33, 35, 38, 40, 44, 46) sts.

Cont working Orchid patt over center front 13 sts for 23 rows, end after working front sts.

Next row: Remove all the markers while working cable patt over next 5 sts, place last 9 sts worked on a st holder or waste yarn, work cable patt on the back, k4 sts past m, place last 9 sts worked on a st holder or waste yarn.

Set sweater body aside.

SLEEVES (Make 2)

With 12"/31 cm circular needles, CO 60 (63, 66, 72, 75, 78, 84) sts, pm, join to work in the rnd, being careful not to twist sts.

Work k2, p1 rib until sleeve measures 1½ (1½, 1½, 1½, 2, 2, 2½)"/3.8 (3.8, 3.8, 3.8, 5, 5, 6.4) cm.

Next rnd: K 1 st past marker, place last 9 sts worked on a holder, remove marker.

Next rnd: To work sleeve sts onto body, sm onto RH longer circular needle, work sleeve sts in rib patt, sm, and work to next st holder.
Set aside.

Repeat for a second sleeve.

There are 4 markers: one on either side of each sleeve. 234 (249, 264, 288, 303, 321, 342) sts.

YOKE

Cont to work rib on sleeve sts, cable patt on back sts, and St st on front sts. Decs will be absorbed into the raglan line.

Rnd 1: **Work to 1 st before m, sl2 k1 p2sso, pm on dec st,** rep between ** 3 more times—8 stitches dec.

Rnd 2: Work even.

Rnd 3: **Work to 1 st before m, sl2 k1 p2sso,** rep between ** 3 more times. Repeat rnds 2 and 3 a total of 20 (21, 22, 24, 25, 26, 28) times—74 (81, 88, 96, 103, 113, 118) sts rem.

Work even for 1"/2.5 cm. BO in patt.

FINISHING

Transfer underarm sts from holders to dpns. Weave underarm sts tog using Kitchener stitch.

Weave in ends. Block sweater to correct measurements.

ORCHID SWEATER SCHEMATIC

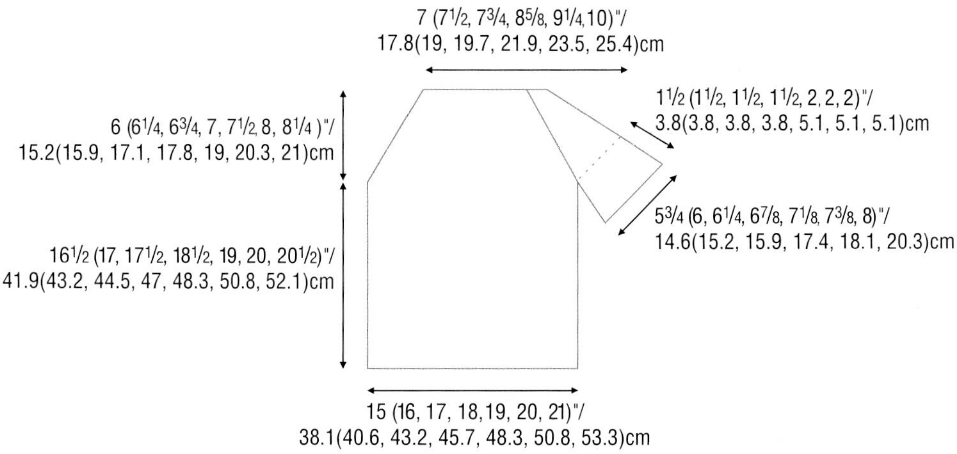
7 (7½, 7¾, 8⅝, 9¼,10)"/
17.8(19, 19.7, 21.9, 23.5, 25.4)cm
1½ (1½, 1½, 1½, 2, 2, 2)"/
3.8(3.8, 3.8, 3.8, 5.1, 5.1, 5.1)cm
6 (6¼, 6¾, 7, 7½, 8, 8¼)"/
15.2(15.9, 17.1, 17.8, 19, 20.3, 21)cm
5¾ (6, 6¼, 6⅞, 7⅛, 7⅜, 8)"/
14.6(15.2, 15.9, 17.4, 18.1, 20.3)cm
16½ (17, 17½, 18½, 19, 20, 20½)"/
41.9(43.2, 44.5, 47, 48.3, 50.8, 52.1)cm
15 (16, 17, 18,19, 20, 21)"/
38.1(40.6, 43.2, 45.7, 48.3, 50.8, 53.3)cm

ENCHANTED CABLES

WAKANA GATES

The cables in this loose-fitting sweater will send any toddler into the world of his favorite fairy tales. The meandering stitch pattern evokes images of magical wonderlands and dream sequences. All the luscious merino cables mirror each other in this artful design, displaying texture and style for your little loved one.

THIS PROJECT WAS KNIT WITH:

Laines Du Nord "Dolly Maxi"
(100% extrafine merino;
95 yd/50 g): 9 (10, 12, 13, 15)
skeins, white (1)

PATTERN NOTES

Circular needles or dpns are not required to knit back, front, and sleeves, but are needed to work collar.

For size 2, the Cable B pattern is worked on 4 sts; for other sizes, Cable B pattern is worked on 6 sts.

When making sleeves, note that the center Cable B patterns should be mirrored; that is, the right sleeve should have the right-slanted Cable B, and the left sleeve should have the left-slanted Cable B.

PATTERN STITCHES

CROSS 2 BACK (C2B)

Multiple of 2 sts.

Insert the rh needle into the front of the second stitch on the lh needle and knit it. *Do not slip off the needle.* K into the front of the first (skipped) stitch, and then slip both stitches off together.

CROSS 2 FRONT (C2F)

Multiple of 2 sts.

Insert the rh needle into the back of the second stitch on the lh needle and knit it. *Do not slip stitch off needle.*

Bring rh needle with stitch on it to front of work and knit the skipped st from the front. Slip both worked stitches off together.

CROSS 6 BACK TWISTED (C6B TWISTED)

Multiple of 6 stitches.

Slip 2 sts onto cable needle and hold at back of work, C2B 2 times in next 4 sts from lh needle, and then C2B 2 sts from cable needle.

SKILL LEVEL

Experienced

SIZE

2 (4, 6, 8, 10)
Shown in size 4

FINISHED MEASUREMENTS

Chest: 28 (30, 31, 32, 34)"/71 (76, 79, 81, 86) cm
Length, collar to hem: 17 (18, 19, 21, 22½)"/43 (46, 48, 53, 57) cm
Sleeve length: 11 (13, 14, 15, 16)"/28 (33, 36, 38, 41) cm

MATERIALS AND TOOLS

Yarn

855 (950, 1140, 1235, 1425) yd/782 (869, 1042, 1129, 1303) m of worsted weight yarn, 100% extrafine merino, in white

Needles

4.5 mm (size 7 U.S.) circular, 24"/61 cm long
5.0 mm (size 8 U.S.) circular, 24"/61 cm long
or size to obtain gauge

Notions

Tapestry needle
Stitch holder
Scrap yarn
Cable needle

GAUGE

24 sts in Cable A pattern = 4"/10.2 cm on 5.0 mm needles
38 rows in Cable A pattern = 5½"/14 cm on 5.0 mm needles

Always take time to check your gauge.

CABLE A PATTERN

24 sts/38 rows

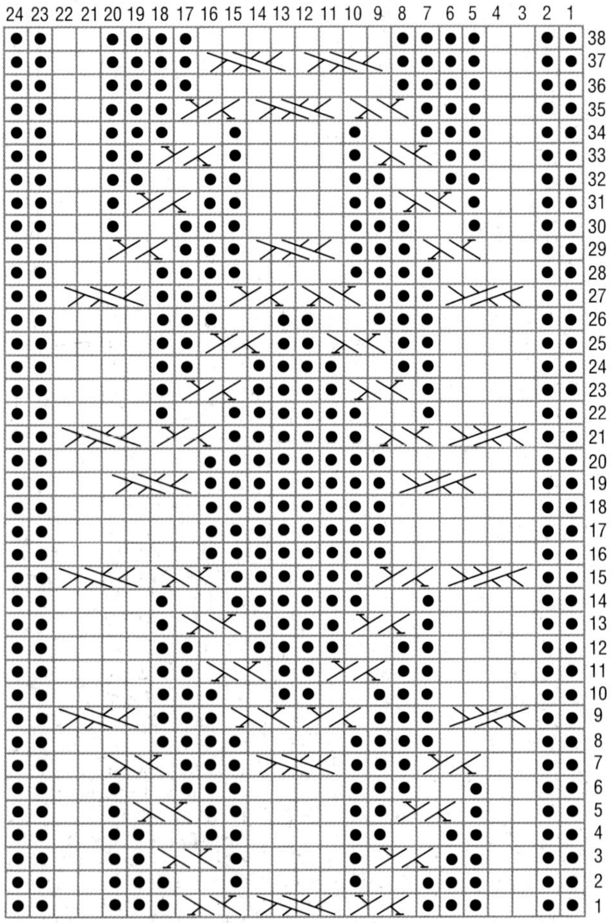

STITCH KEY

RS: Knit
WS: Purl

RS: Purl
WS: Knit

C4B (Cable 4 Back)

C4F (Cable 4 Front)

T3B (Twist 3 Back)

T3F (Twist 3 Front)

CABLE B PATTERN

Multiple of 6 sts (4 sts for smallest size) on 12 rows

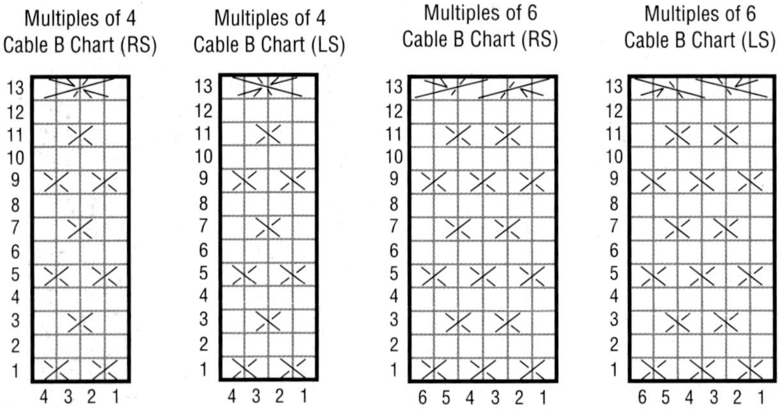
Multiples of 4
Cable B Chart (RS)
Multiples of 4
Cable B Chart (LS)
Multiples of 6
Cable B Chart (RS)
Multiples of 6
Cable B Chart (LS)

STITCH KEY

C2B (Cross 2 Back)

C2F (Cross 2 Front)

C4B Twisted
(Cross 4 Twisted Back)

C4F Twisted
(Cross 4 Twisted Front)

RS: Knit
WS: Purl

Highlighted Repeat

C6B Twisted
(Cross 6 Front Twisted)

C6F Twisted
(Cross 6 Front Twisted)

CROSS 6 FRONT TWISTED (C6F TWISTED)

Multiple of 6 sts.

Slip 4 sts onto cable needle and hold at front of work, C2F 2 times in next 4 sts from lh needle, and then C2F 2 sts from cable needle.

CROSS 4 BACK TWISTED (C4B TWISTED)

Multiple of 4 sts.

Slip next 2 sts onto cable needle and hold at back of work, C2B next 2 sts from lh needle, and then C2B 2 sts from cable needle

CROSS 4 FRONT TWISTED (C4F TWISTED)

Multiple of 4 sts.

Slip next 2 sts onto cable needle and hold at front of work, C2F next 2 sts from lh needle, then C2F 2 sts from cable needle.

TWIST 3 BACK (T3B)

Slip next st onto cable needle and hold at back of work, k2 from lh needle, then p1 from cable needle.

TWIST 3 FRONT (T3F)

Slip next 2 sts onto cable needle and hold at front of work, p1 from lh needle, then k2 from cable needle.

CABLE C PATTERN (PLAITED BASKET STITCH)

Multiple of 8 sts on 2 rows.

Row 1 (RS): *K the second stitch on the lh needle from the back, then k the first stitch from the front, rep from * 3 more times.

Row 2 (WS): P1, **p the second stitch and then p the first stitch**, rep between ** 2 more times, p1.

Rep rows 1–2.

INSTRUCTIONS

BACK

With 4.5 mm needle, CO 82 (88, 90, 94, 100) sts.

Row 1 (WS): P2, *k1, p1, rep from * to end.

Row 2 (RS): P3 (2, 3, 3, 6), k4 (6, 6, 6, 6) for Cable B, [p2, k2, p4, k8, p4, k2, p2] for Cable A, k4 (6, 6, 6, 6) for Cable B, p3 (2, 3, 3, 3), k6 (8, 8, 8, 10, 10) for Cable C, p3 (2, 2, 3, 3), k4 (6, 6, 6, 6) for Cable B, [p2, k2, p4, k8, p4, k2, p2] for Cable A, k4 (6, 6, 6, 6) for Cable B, p3 (2, 3, 3, 6).

Change to 5.0 mm needle.

Row 3 (WS): K3 (2, 3, 3, 6), p4 (6, 6, 6, 6), k2, p2, k4, p8, k4, p2, k2, p4 (6, 6, 6, 6), k3 (2, 3, 3, 3), p6 (8, 8, 8, 10, 10), k3 (2, 2, 3, 3), p4 (6, 6, 6, 6), k2, p2, k4, p8, k4, p2, k2, p4 (6, 6, 6, 6), p3 (2, 3, 3, 6).

Work even in patt (see cable placement chart) for 54 (66, 72, 84, 92) rows and piece measures 10 (12, 13, 15, 16½)"/25 (30.5, 33, 38.1, 41.9) cm from CO.

RAGLAN DECREASE

P1, k2tog (or p2tog if the third st is purl st), work in patt st to 3 sts before end, ssk (or ssp if the third to last st is purl st), p1.

Repeat dec row every row 26 (28, 29, 30, 32) times.

Next row: BO 30 (32, 32, 34, 36) sts.

FRONT

Work same as back until 10th row of Raglan Decrease, ending with WS row—62 (68, 70, 74, 80) sts.

Right Front

Cont working cable pattern and raglan dec as established, working left and right fronts separately as follows.

Work 27 (30, 31, 33, 36) sts, place next 6 sts on st holder for neck opening, work 28 (31, 32, 34, 37) sts for right front. Left and right fronts are worked separately.

Work raglan dec on next 7 rows, ending with a WS row—20 (23, 24, 26, 29) sts rem.

Then, dec 1 st each side every row for 6 (9, 10, 11, 13) rows—8 (5, 4, 4, 3) sts rem.

Size 2 Only

Next row (RS): K2tog twice, ssk 2 times—4 sts rem.

Next row (WS): P2tog, ssp—2 sts rem.

Next row (RS): K2tog. Fasten off.

Size 4 Only

Next row (WS): P1, p3tog, p1—3 sts rem.

Next row (RS): K3tog. Fasten off.

Size 6 Only

Next row (RS): K2tog, ssk—2 sts rem.

Next row (WS): P2tog. Fasten off.

Size 8 Only

Next row (WS): P2 tog, ssp—2 sts rem.

Next row (RS): K2tog. Fasten off.

Size 10 Only

Next row (WS): P3tog. Fasten off.

Left Front (All Sizes)

Work same as Right Front.

SLEEVES (Make 2)

With 4.5 mm needle, CO 52 (54, 56, 58, 62) sts.

Row 1 (WS): P2, *k1, p1, rep from * to end.

Size 2 (4, 6) Only

Row 2 (RS): K0 (0, 1) for Cable B, (p2, k4, p4, k4, p4, k4, p2) for Cable A, k4 (6, 6) for Cable B, (p2, k4, p4, k4, p4, k4, p2) for Cable A, k0 (0, 1) for Cable B.

Change to 5.0 mm needle.

Row 3 (WS): P0 (0, 1), k2, p4, k4, p4, k4, p4, k2, p4 (6, 6), k2, p4, k4, p4, k4, p4, k2, p0 (0, 1).

Size 8 (10) Only

Row 2 (RS): K2 (4) for Cable B, (p5, k2, p3, k4, p3, k2, p5) for Cable A, k6 for Cable B, (p5, k2, p3, k4, p3, k2, p5) for Cable A, k2 (4) for Cable B.

Change to 5.0 mm needle.

Row 3 (WS): P2 (4), k5, p2, k3, p4, k3, p2, k5, p6, k5, p2, k3, p4, k3, p2, k5, p2 (4).

For All Sizes

Beg with row 29 (29, 29, 33, 33) on Cable A chart, cont working in patt for 64 (76, 82, 88, 98) rows.

AT THE SAME TIME, inc 1 st each side every 8 (8, 8, 8, 10, 10) rows 7 (8, 8, 8, 9) times—66 (70, 72, 74, 80) sts.

Raglan Decrease

Dec 1 st each side every row for 26 (28, 29, 30, 32) rows as follows.

P1, k2 tog (or p2tog if the third st is purl st), cont in pattern stitch to 3 sts before end, ssk (or ssp if the third to last st is purl st), p1.

Next row: BO 14 (14, 14, 14, 16) sts.

FINISHING

Block to size.

Sew sleeves to front and back along raglan line. Sew side and sleeve seams together in one continuous seam.

Collar

With 4.5 mm needle and RS facing, p/u 8 sts from center opening, 10 (12, 13, 14, 16) sts from right front, 12 (12, 12, 12, 14) sts from sleeve, 28 (30, 30, 32, 34) sts from back, 12 (12, 12, 12, 14) sts from sleeve, 10 (12, 13, 14, 16) sts from left front, and 8 sts from center opening—88 (94, 96, 100, 110) sts.

Row 1 (WS): *P2, k1, rep from * to 2 sts before end, p2, CO 1 (1, 0, 1, 1) st—89 (95, 96, 101, 111) sts.

Row 2 (RS): K to end.

Row 3 (WS): *P2, k1, rep from * to 2 sts before end, p2.

Rep rows 2–3 two more times.

Row 8 (RS): BO 8 sts, k to end.

Row 9 (WS): BO 8 sts pwise, *p2, k1, rep from * to 3 sts before end, p3.

Rep rows 2–3 4 (6, 7, 8, 9) more times.

Next row (WS): K to end.

Next row (RS): K to end.

Rep rows 2–3 8 (10, 11, 12, 13) more times.

Cut yarn, leaving a 60"/152.4 cm-long tail.

Fold collar in half with WS tog and sew the last row onto the first row.

Invisibly sew side of collar closed.

Move 6 sts from st holder to 5.0 mm needle. Sew those sts to bottom of left front opening on the inside. Place right front opening on top of left front opening and sew tog.

ENCHANTED CABLES SCHEMATIC

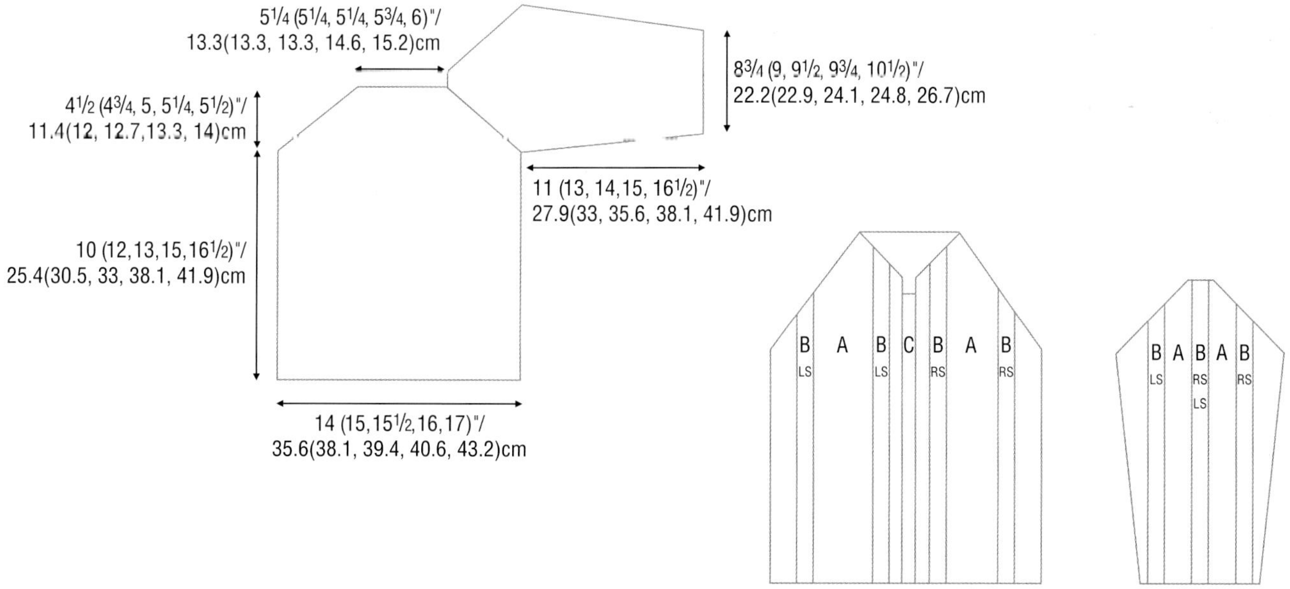

5 1/4 (5 1/4, 5 1/4, 5 3/4, 6)"/ 13.3(13.3, 13.3, 14.6, 15.2)cm
4 1/2 (4 3/4, 5, 5 1/4, 5 1/2)"/ 11.4(12, 12.7,13.3, 14)cm
8 3/4 (9, 9 1/2, 9 3/4, 10 1/2)"/ 22.2(22.9, 24.1, 24.8, 26.7)cm
11 (13, 14,15, 16 1/2)"/ 27.9(33, 35.6, 38.1, 41.9)cm
10 (12,13,15,16 1/2)"/ 25.4(30.5, 33, 38.1, 41.9)cm
14 (15,15 1/2,16,17)"/ 35.6(38.1, 39.4, 40.6, 43.2)cm
B A B C B A B
LS LS RS RS
B A B A B
LS RS RS
LS

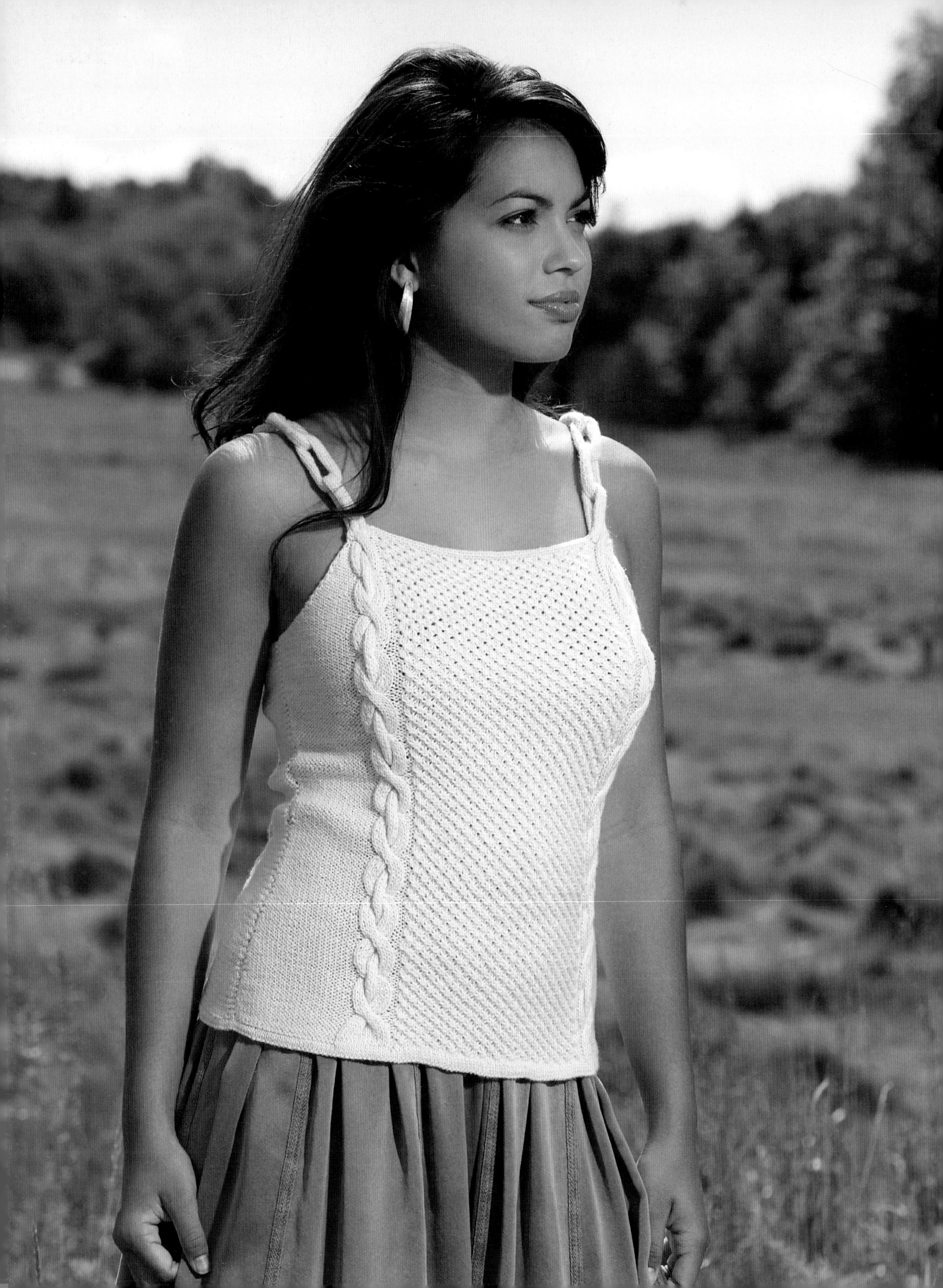

CHAINS OF LOVE CAMISOLE

OLGA BURAYA-KEFELIAN

The chain-linked cables transitioning into chained I-cord straps draw immediate attention to this elegant cami, while the daisy stitch center panel creates a textured depth.

SKILL LEVEL

Experienced

SIZES

XS (S, M, L, XL)
30 (34, 38, 42, 46)"/
76 (86, 97, 107, 117) cm
Shown in size S

FINISHED MEASUREMENTS

Chest: 28 (32, 36, 40, 44)"/
71 (81, 91, 102, 112) cm
Length: 21½ (22, 23, 24, 25)"/
55 (55, 58, 61, 64) cm

MATERIALS AND TOOLS

Yarn

675 (810, 945, 945, 1080) yd/
617 (741, 864, 864, 988) m of worsted weight yarn, 33% wool, 33% silk, 33% milk protein, in natural

Needles

3.25 mm (size 3 U.S.)
circular, 24"/61 cm long
2.75 mm (size 2 U.S.)
circular, 24"/61 cm long
2.75 mm (size 2 U.S.) dpns
or size to obtain gauge

Notions

2 cable needles
Tapestry needle
Waste yarn
4 stitch holders

GAUGE

26 sts and 38 rows = 4"/10.2 cm
in St st on 3.25 mm needles

Always take time to check your gauge.

THIS PROJECT WAS KNIT WITH:

Tilli Tomas Elsie (33% wool, 33% silk, 33% milk protein; 135 yd/ 50 g): 5 (6, 7, 7, 8) skeins, Natural

4

PATTERN STITCHES

STAR STITCH

Multiple of 4 sts plus 1 st; 4 row repeat.

Row 1 (RS): **K3tog (do not take sts off needle), yo and k1 through same 3 sts, k1**, rep between ** to last stitch. K1.

Row 2: P.

Row 3: K1, **k1, k3tog (do not take sts off needle), yo and k1 through same 3 sts**, rep between ** to end.

Row 4: P.

LEFT-SIDE CABLE

Row 1: Sl4 sts to cn and hold in back of work, sl next 4 sts to second cn and hold in back of work, k4 sts from left needle, pass first cable needle through to front of work, k4 sts from second cable needle, then k4 from first cable needle.

Rows 2–12: Work even.

Row 13: Sl4 sts to cn and hold in back of work, sl next 4 sts to second cn and hold in front of work, k4 sts from left needle, then k4 from second cn, then k4 from first cn.

Rows 14–24: Work even.

Rep rows 1–24 for pattern.

RIGHT-SIDE CABLE

Row 1: Sl4 sts to cn and hold in front of work, sl next 4 sts to second cn and hold in back of work, k4 sts from left needle, then k4 from second cn, then k4 from first cn.

Rows 2–12: Work even.

Row 13: Sl4 sts to cn and hold in front of work, sl next 4 sts to second cn and hold in front of work, k4 from left needle, pass first cn through to back of work, k4 from second cn, then k4 from first cn.

INSTRUCTIONS

FRONT

Hem

With provisional or invisible cast on, 2.75 mm needles, and waste yarn, CO 115 (131, 147, 163, 179) sts.

Change to main yarn and work 4 rows in St st.

P 1 row (hem turning row).

Work 5 more rows in St st.

Fold work along p row with WS tog and k1 st from needle with 1 st from CO row to end.

Change to 3.25 mm needles.

Row 1 (WS): K19 (24, 29, 33, 37), p12, k2, p49 (55, 61, 69, 77), k2, p12, k19 (24, 29, 33, 37) sts.

Rows 2–5: Work even beg Star Stitch on center 49 (55, 61, 69, 77) sts.

Work evenly in patt until piece measures 1½"/3.8 cm from hem edge.

Beg working right and left cables on both 19 (24, 29, 33, 37) st sections.

Work evenly in patt until piece measures 2 (2¼, 2½, 2¾, 3)"/5.1(5.7, 6.4, 7, 7.6) cm from the hem edge.

Waist Shaping

Row 1 (Dec): K1, ssk, work to last 3 sts, k2tog, k1.

Work 5 (5, 5, 6, 6) rows even.

Rep the last 6 (6, 6, 7, 7) rows 4 (5, 6, 6, 7) more times—10 (12, 14, 14, 16) sts dec; 105 (119, 133, 149, 163) sts rem. Work even for 1 (1¾, 2, 2¼, 2½)"/ 2.5 (4.4, 5.1, 5.7, 6.4) cm.

Inc Row: K1, k1fb, rep to last 2 sts, k1fb, k1.

Work 13 (12, 11, 10, 9) rows even.

Rep the last 14 (13, 12, 11, 10) rows 2 (3, 4, 4, 5) more times—6 (8, 10, 10, 12) sts inc; 111 (127, 143, 159, 175) sts rem.

Work even until piece measures 13½ (13½, 14, 14¾, 15½)"/34 (34, 36, 37, 39) cm from hem edge.

Armhole Shaping

***Note:** When there are 2 decs, split decs between current row and next row to create a smoother dec line.*

Row 1: BO 4 (5, 6, 7, 8) sts at beg of next 2 rows.

Row 3: Dec 2 (2, 3, 3, 3) sts at beg and end of row.

Row 5: Dec 1 (2, 2, 3, 3) sts at beg and end of row.

Row 7: Dec 1 (2, 2, 2, 2) sts at beg and end of row.

Row 9: Dec 1 (1, 2, 2, 2) sts at beg and end of row.

Row 11: Dec 1 (1, 1, 1, 1) sts at beg and end of row.

Row 13: Dec 1 (1, 1, 1, 1) sts at beg and end of row.

Row 15: Dec 1 (1, 1, 1, 1) sts at beg and end of row.

Row 17: Dec 1 (1, 1, 1, 1) sts at beg and end of row.

Row 19: Dec 1 (1, 1, 1, 1) sts at beg and end of row.

Row 21: Dec 1 (1, 1, 1, 1) sts at beg and end of row.

Row 23: Dec 1 (1, 1, 1, 1) sts at beg and end of row.

Row 25: Dec 0 (1, 1, 1, 1) sts at beg and end of row.

Row 27: Dec 0 (0, 1, 1, 1) sts at beg and end of row.

Row 29: Dec 0 (0, 1, 1, 1) sts at beg and end of row.

Row 31: Dec 0 (0, 1, 1, 1) sts at beg and end of row.

Row 33: Dec 0 (0, 0, 1, 1) sts at beg and end of row.

Row 35: Dec 0 (0, 0, 1, 1) sts at beg and end of row.

Row 37: Dec 0 (0, 0, 0, 1) sts at beg and end of row.

Row 39: Dec 0 (0, 0, 0, 1) sts at beg and end of row.

16 (20, 26, 30, 33) sts dec on each side.

Place rem 95 (107, 117, 129, 142) sts on a holder or waste yarn.

BACK

Work as for front up to armhole shaping.

Armhole Shaping

Row 1: BO 4 (5, 6, 7, 8) sts at beg of next 2 rows.

Row 3: Dec 2 (3, 3, 4, 4) sts at beg and end of row.

Row 5: Dec 2 (2, 3, 3, 3) sts at beg and end of row.

Row 7: Dec 2 (2, 2, 3, 3) sts at beg and end of row.

Row 9: Dec 2 (2, 2, 2, 2) sts at beg and end of row.

Row 11: Dec 2 (2, 2, 2, 2) sts at beg and end of row.

Row 13: Dec 2 (2, 2, 2, 2) sts at beg and end of row.

Row 15: Dec 0 (1, 2, 2, 2) sts at beg and end of row.

Row 17: Dec 0 (1, 2, 2, 2) sts at beg and end of row.

Row 19: Dec 0 (0, 1, 1, 2) sts at beg and end of row.

Row 21: Dec 0 (0, 1, 1, 1) sts at beg and end of row.

Row 23: Dec 0 (0, 0, 1, 1) sts at beg and end of row.

Row 25: Dec 0 (0, 0, 0, 1) sts at beg and end of row.

16 (20, 26, 30, 33) sts dec on each side. Place rem 95 (107, 117, 129, 142) sts on holder or waste yarn.

I-Cord Bind Off

Place all sts back from stitch holder or waste yarn on smaller needle.

Dec for the strap (make 7 from 14 sts): k2tog 3 times, ssk 4 times, put those 7 sts aside on a stitch holder.

With 2.75 mm dpn, p/u 2 sts from the corner right in front of remaining sts on the needle and make the I-cord BO as follows.

K2, slip 1 kwise, k1, psso, slide the sts on rh needle to other end of needle, rep between **, being sure to tighten the first st of each new row. Rep until 14 sts rem.

K2tog 4 times, ssk 3 times. Place rem sts on st holder.

FINISHING

Move 7 sts from holder to 2.75 mm needles and work I-cord for 3½ (3¾, 4, 4¼, 4½)"/8.9 (9.5, 10.2, 10.8, 11.4) cm. With sts still on needle, fold I-cord in half and graft live sts to the inside of the camisole at the base of the strap. Rep with other 3 straps coming off the body.

Individual I-cord chain links: Using provisional cast on and scrap yarn, CO 7 sts. Work I-cord as above, insert the completed link into other link, unravel provisional cast on edge sts one by one, and graft together.

Chain Links Shoulder Straps (Make 10)

With provisionsal or invisible CO, using 2.75 mm dpns and waste yarn, CO 7 sts. Change to main yarn and make I-cord as follows.

K 1 row, slide knitting to other end of needle. Knit row 2, being sure to tighten the 1st st of each new row.

Work until I-cord measures 3½ (3¾, 4, 4¼, 4¼)"/8.9 (9.5, 10.2, 10.8, 10.8) cm and transfer to a st holder.

To join link, unravel stitches from provisional CO and place on needle. With tapestry needle, graft both edges of I-cord together (or to top edge of camisole), being careful not to twist and securing ends on inside. To join 2 links, insert one link through another and then graft, being careful not to twist cord.

Make 10 I-cord stripes (5 for each chain link strap), attaching them as described above.

Seaming

Sew side seams tog with mattress stitch. Weave in ends.

Block to size.

CHAINS OF LOVE CAMISOLE SCHEMATIC

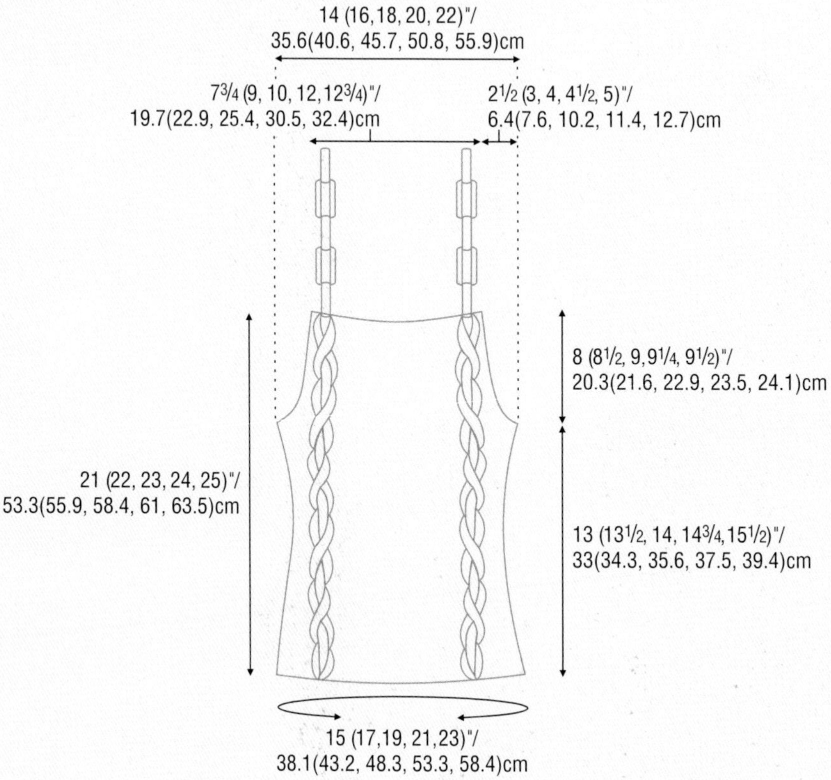
14 (16, 18, 20, 22)"/
35.6(40.6, 45.7, 50.8, 55.9)cm
7¾ (9, 10, 12, 12¾)"/
19.7(22.9, 25.4, 30.5, 32.4)cm
2½ (3, 4, 4½, 5)"/
6.4(7.6, 10.2, 11.4, 12.7)cm
8 (8½, 9, 9¼, 9½)"/
20.3(21.6, 22.9, 23.5, 24.1)cm
21 (22, 23, 24, 25)"/
53.3(55.9, 58.4, 61, 63.5)cm
13 (13½, 14, 14¾, 15½)"/
33(34.3, 35.6, 37.5, 39.4)cm
15 (17, 19, 21, 23)"/
38.1(43.2, 48.3, 53.3, 58.4)cm

ISAAC'S ARAN

LEAH BEAR

The idea of a classic fisherman's Aran is updated with a closer fit, and knit with sumptuous yarn. The light loft of the Malabrigo pairs perfectly with the rich texture of the seed stitch and shows off the cable stitches beautifully. The seed stitch is changed to knit 2, purl 2, ribbing at an angle, giving the illusion of shaping without any. This sweater is knit seamlessly in the round for a professionally finished look.

SKILL LEVEL
Experienced

SIZES
S (M, L XL)
38 (42, 46, 50)"/97 (107, 117, 127) cm
Shown in size M

FINISHED MEASUREMENTS
Chest: 39 (43, 47, 51)"/99 (109, 119, 130) cm
Body length: 16 (17, 18, 19)"/
41 (43, 46, 48) cm
Sleeve length: 18 (19, 20, 20½)"/
46 (48, 51, 52) cm

MATERIALS AND TOOLS

Yarn
1290 (1505, 1720, 1935) yd/1180 (1376, 1573, 1769) m of worsted weight yarn, 100% merino wool, in natural

Needles
4.5 mm (size 7 U.S.) circular, 40"/102 cm long
4.5 mm (size 7 U.S.) dpns
or size to obtain gauge

Notions
Cable needle
Tapestry needle
Scrap yarn
Stitch markers

GAUGE
20 sts and 36 rows = 4"/
10.2 cm in Seed st

Always take time to check your gauge.

THIS PROJECT WAS KNIT WITH:
Malabrigo Merino Worsted
(100% merino wool; 215 yd/100 g):
6 (7, 8, 9) skeins, Natural (63)

PATTERN STITCHES

FRONT CABLE (FC)
Slip 2 sts to a cable needle and hold in front of work, p1 st, then k2 sts from cable needle.

BACK CABLE (BC)
Slip 1 stitch to a cable needle and hold in back of work, k2 sts, then purl 1st from cable needle.

YO, K2, PASS YO OVER K 2 STS
Yarn over, knit 2 stiches, then pass yo over 2 knit stitches.

CABLE 1 OVER 2 RIGHT (C1-2R)
Slip 2 stitches to cable needle, hold in back, knit 1, then knit 2 from cable needle.

CABLE 1 OVER 2 LEFT (C1-2L)
Slip 1 stitch to cable needle, hold in front, knit 2, then knit 1 from cable needle.

CABLE 2 OVER 2 RIGHT (C2 -2R)
Slip 2 stitches to cable needle, hold in back, knit 2, then knit 2 from cable needle.

CABLE 2 OVER 2 LEFT (C2-2L)
Slip 2 stitches to cable needle, hold in front, knit 2, then knit 2 from cable needle.

INSTRUCTIONS

BODY
With circular needles and long-tail cast on, CO 196, (216, 236, 256) sts, pm, and join to k in the rnd, being careful not to twist sts.

Work even in k2, p2 rib until work measures 2"/15 cm from CO.

Begin working in patt as follows.

Rnd 1: K29 (34, 39, 44) sts in Seed st, pm, 1st row of cable pattern on 43 sts, pm, k58 (68, 78, 88) sts in Seed st, pm, work first row of cable pattern on 43 sts, k29 (34, 39, 44) sts in Seed st.

Work even in established patt following instructions for cables and Seed st until piece measures 11 (12, 13, 14)"/28 (30, 33, 36) cm from CO, ending with rnd 12 of cable patt.

Begin Ribbing
Work Seed st to 1 st before first cable pattern marker, k1, slip marker, work 43 sts of cable pattern, slip marker, k1, work Seed st to 1 st before next marker, k1, slip marker, work 43 sts of cable pattern, slip marker, k1, work in Seed st to end of round.

Cont working in pattern as established, working 1 more st at edge of Seed st panels into k2, p2 pattern on each round, resulting in k2, p2 rib replacing Seed sts.

Work until all Seed sts have become k2, p2 rib and work measures 16 (17, 18, 19)"/41 (43, 46, 48) cm from CO, ending the last rnd 5 (5, 7, 7) sts before beg of rnd marker and ending with either row 3, 7, or 11 of the cable patt.

SEED STITCH

Rnd 1: *K1, p1, rep from *.

Rnd 2: *P1, k1, rep from *.

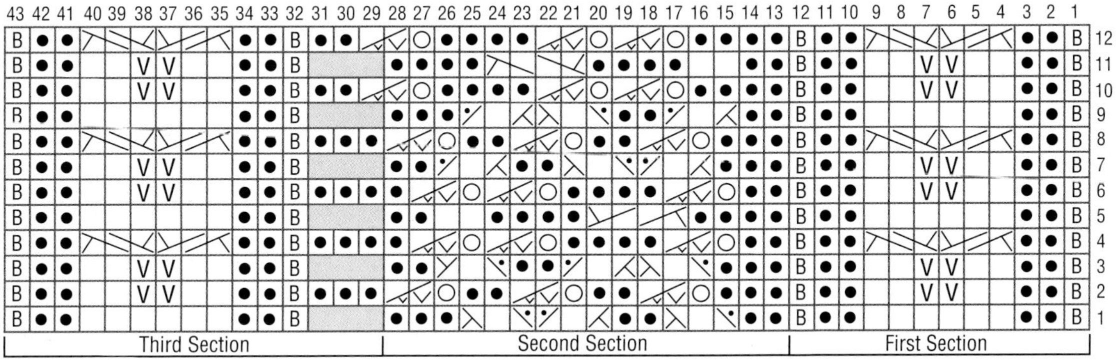
Third Section
Second Section
First Section

STITCH KEY

B — Knit tbl
Knit through back loop.

Front Cable (FC)
Sl2 onto CN, hold in front, p1, K2 from CN.

Back Cable (BC)
Sl1 onto CN, hold in back. K2, P1 from CN.

C2 over 2 left
Sl2 onto CN, hold in front. K2, K2 from CN.

C2 over 2 right
Sl2 to CN, hold in back. K2, K2 from CN.

C1 over 2 right
Sl2 to CN, hold in back, K1, k2 from CN.

C1 over 2 left
Sl1 to CN, hold in front. K2, k1 from CN.

Knit
Knit stitch.

No stitch
Placeholder- no stitch made.

Purl
Purl stitch.

Yarn over, K2, pass the yo over.

V — Slip
Slip stitch as if to purl, holding yarn at back.

DIVIDE FOR FRONT & BACK

BO 10 (10, 14, 14) sts, work 88 (98, 104, 114) in patt, BO 10 (10, 14, 14) sts, work 88 (98, 104, 114) in patt—176 (196, 208, 228) sts rem.

Set aside and note which row of the cable pattern was just completed.

SLEEVES (Make 2)

With long-tail cast on and dpns, CO 30 (36, 42, 52) sts, pm, and join to work in the rnd.

Work in k2, p2 rib until work measures 2"/5 cm from CO.

Change to Seed st and inc 1 st each side of the m every 10 (10, 8, 8) rnds, 6 (6, 7, 7) times.

Then, inc 1 st each side of the m every 5 (5, 4, 4) rnds, 9 (12, 12, 12) times—60 (72, 80, 90) sts rem.

Work even in Seed st until work measures 18 (19, 20, 20½)"/46 (48, 51, 52) cm from beg or to desired length, ending 5 (5, 7, 7) sts before marker, BO 10 (10, 14, 14) sts, work to end of rnd.

50 (62, 66, 76) sts rem. Place sts on st holder or waste yarn and set aside.

Work the second sleeve as the first.

Yoke

With RS facing, cont working in pattern and join pieces as follows.

Rnd 1: Work 88 (98, 104, 114) sts across front, pm, work 50 (62, 66, 76) sts of left sleeve, pm, work 88 (98, 104, 114) sts from back, pm, and work 48 (62, 72, 78) sts of right sleeve, pm to mark end of rnd—276 (320, 340, 380) total sts.

Raglan Shaping

Rnd 2: **K2tog, k in patt to 2 sts before m, ssk, sm,** rep between ** 3 times—8 sts dec.

Rnds 3–5: Work even in patt.

Rep rnds 2–5 3 (2, 1, 0) times—244 (296, 324, 372) stitches rem.

Rep dec rnds 2–3 20 (23, 26, 29) more times—84 (112, 116, 140) stitches rem.

AT THE SAME TIME, when yoke measures 6½ (7½, 7½, 8)"/17 (19, 19, 20) cm from join, beg neck shaping as follows.

BO 12 (14, 16, 16) sts at center front and work to end.

Beg working back and forth in patt, cont raglan dec each WS row as follows: **P to 2 sts before m, p2tog, sm, ssk,** rep between ** 3 more times, and BO 3 sts at each neck edge 1 (2, 2, 2) times—66 (86, 88, 112) sts rem.

BO all stitches loosely.

With dpns or the 40"/102 cm circular needle, (using magic loop method, page 135), p/u and k54—88 (96, 108, 120) sts at neckline.

Work in k2, p2 rib for 1"/2.5 cm. BO all sts loosely in rib.

FINISHING

Sew underarms. Weave in ends.

Block sweater.

ISAAC'S ARAN SCHEMATIC

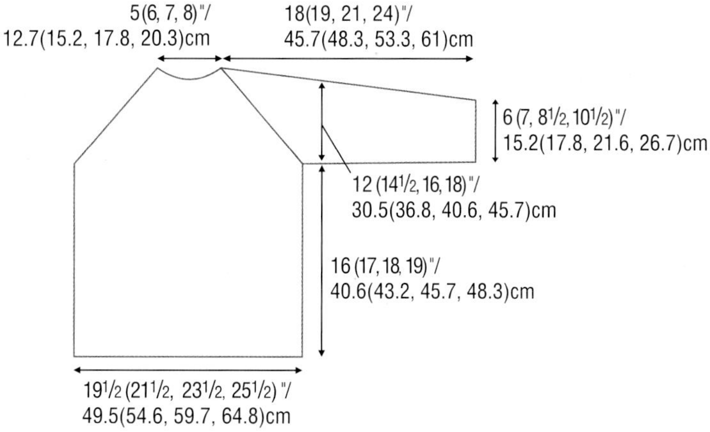
5(6, 7, 8)"/
12.7(15.2, 17.8, 20.3)cm
18(19, 21, 24)"/
45.7(48.3, 53.3, 61)cm
6 (7, 8½, 10½)"/
15.2(17.8, 21.6, 26.7)cm
12 (14½, 16, 18)"/
30.5(36.8, 40.6, 45.7)cm
16 (17, 18, 19)"/
40.6(43.2, 45.7, 48.3)cm
19½ (21½, 23½, 25½)"/
49.5(54.6, 59.7, 64.8)cm

FUTURE ARAN

YAHAIRA FERREIRA

A companion to Isaac's Aran, this sweater updates the tradition of Aran knits with a modern fit and look. Using a chunky merino blend, the allover cables seem to pop off the cartridge rib background. The merino and perendale work together to create a balance between the softness and ruggedness of the sweater. The slimmer fit and funnel neck give the look a futuristic edge that is enhanced by the white color.

THIS PROJECT WAS KNIT WITH:

Pear Tree Summit (60% merino wool, 40% perendale wool; 170 yd/100 g): 7 (7, 8, 8, 9) skeins, Natural

5

PATTERN NOTES

Body rounds begin at the back raglan line to allow for easier stitch count placement.

Work increased sleeve stitches into cartridge rib, maintaining first and last stitches.

Before joining, be sure to end body and sleeves on same round.

On yoke and funnel neck, work a selvedge of 2 knit stitches on the sleeve side of the raglan line and a selvedge of purl 1, knit 2 on the body sides of the raglan line.

As stitches are decreased along the raglan line, work partial or half cables at sides as the stitch count allows. On sleeve, continue to work cable until 12 stitches remain, ending on a twist round.

SPECIAL ABBREVIATIONS

6-St LC: slip 3 stitches to cable needle and hold in front of work, knit 3, knit 3 from cable needle.

6-St RC: slip 3 stitches to cable needle and hold in back of work, knit 3, knit 3 from cable needle.

PATTERN STITCHES

CARTRIDGE RIB (CR)

Multiple of 5, plus 2 in the round.

Rnd 1: P1, k2, *p1, k4, rep from * last to last 3 sts, and end with k2, p1.

Rnd 2: P1, k1, *p3, k2, rep from * to last 2 sts, and end with k1, p1.

UPSIDE DOWN HORSESHOE (HC)

Multiple of 12 sts in the round.

Rnds 1–4: Knit all sts.

Rnds 5: 6-St LC, 6-St RC.

Rnd 6: Knit.

Rep rnds 1–6.

SKILL LEVEL

Experienced

SIZES

XS (S, M, L, XL)
36 (42, 45, 48, 50)"/
91 (107, 114, 122, 127) cm
Shown in size S

FINISHED MEASUREMENTS

Chest: 38¼ (44, 47, 50, 52½)"/
97 (112, 119, 127, 133) cm
Length: 24 (25, 26, 26½, 27½)"/
61 (64, 66, 67, 70) cm
Sleeve length: 18½ (19, 19½, 19½, 20)"/47 (48, 50, 50, 51) cm

MATERIALS AND TOOLS

Yarn

1190 (1190, 1360, 1360, 1530) yd/
1088 (1088, 1244, 1244, 1399) m of chunky weight yarn, 60% merino wool, 40% perendale wool, in natural

Needles

6.5 mm (size 10½ U.S.) circular, 32"/81 cm long and dpns
7.0 mm (size 10.75 U.S.) circular, 32"/81 cm long and dpns
or size to obtain gauge

Notions

Stitch markers
Stitch holder
Cable needle
Tapestry needle

GAUGE

14 sts and 20 rows = 4"/10.2 cm in Cartridge Rib on 7.0 mm needles

Always take time to check your gauge.

INSTRUCTIONS

BODY

With 6.5 mm needle, CO 132 (152, 160, 172, 180) sts, pm, and join to work in the rnd, being careful not to twist sts.

Work in k2, p2 rib until piece measures 3"/7.6 cm from CO.

Change to 7.0 mm needle and work in patt as described below. And AT THE SAME TIME, inc 2 (2, 4, 2, 4) sts evenly across rnd—134 (154, 164, 174, 184) sts total.

Work pattern stitches as follows.

XS: *7 CR, 12 HC, 12 CR, 12 HC, 12 CR, 12 HC, pm, rep from * to end.

S: *17 CR, 12 HC, 12 CR, 12 HC, 12 CR, 12 HC, pm, rep from * to end.

M: *12 CR, 12 HC, 17 CR, 12 HC, 17 CR, 12 HC, pm, rep from * to end.

L: *17 CR, 12 HC, 17 CR, 12 HC, 17 CR, 12 HC, pm, rep from * to end.

XL: *22 CR, 12 HC, 17 CR, 12 HC, 17 CR, 12 HC, pm, rep from * to end.

Work even until piece measures 12 (13, 13 ¼, 13½, 13 ½)"/30.5 (33, 33.7, 34.3, 34.3) cm from CO.

Divide for Yoke

Work 7 (12, 10, 13, 16) sts, place the last 7 (7, 8, 9, 10) sts worked on a st holder, work to 7 (12, 10, 13, 16) sts past next marker, place the last 7 (7, 8, 9, 10) sts worked on st holder, work to end of rnd (front)—120 (140, 148, 154, 164) sts rem. Set work aside, and do not break yarn.

SLEEVES (Make 2)

With 6.5 mm dpns, CO 32 (32, 32, 36, 36) sts, pm, and join to work in the rnd.

Work in k2, p2 rib until piece measures 3"/7.6 cm from CO.

Change to 7.0 mm dpns and work in patt, working 12 center sts in cable pattern as follows.

XS, S, M, only: 10 CR, 12 HC, 10 CR.

L, XL only: 12 CR, 12 HC, 12 CR.

AT THE SAME TIME, inc 4 (4, 4, 0, 0) sts evenly across next round—36 (36, 36, 36, 36) sts.

Inc Rnd: K1, m1l, k to last two sts, m1r, k1.

Work inc rnd every 9 (7, 6, 6 ,6) rnds 7 (7, 7, 10, 3) times, then every 0 (8, 5, 5 , 5) rnds 0 (2, 4, 2, 11) times—50 (54, 58, 60, 64) sts rem.

Work even until sleeve measures 15½ (16, 16½, 16¾, 17)"/39 (41, 42, 43, 43) cm from hem.

Next rnd: K4 (4, 5, 5, 5), place the last 7 (7, 10, 10, 10) sts worked on a st holder, work to end—43 (47, 50, 50, 54) sts rem. Break yarn.

Work the sleeve sts onto the circular needle for the body next to the 60 (70, 74, 78, 82) sts for front, pm, then work the 60 (70, 74, 78, 82) sts for the back.

Set work aside.

Work the second sleeve as the first.

Yoke

Work 43 (47, 50, 50, 54) sts of left sleeve onto circular needle next to sts for back, pm, work 60 (70, 74, 77, 82) sts for front, pm to mark beg of rnd and right raglan line (use different color marker).

Work 2 rnds even, working in patt as established, ending last round 4 sts before m.

Dec Rnd: *Ssk, k1, p1, pm, k1, k2tog, k to within 3 sts of next marker, ssk, k1, pm, p1, k1, k2tog; rep from * 2 more times—8 sts dec; 198 (226, 240, 246, 264) sts rem.

Sizes XS and S

Rep front/back dec rnd every 3 (3) rnds 8 (9) times more and then every 2 (2) rnds 6 (7) times. AT THE SAME TIME, rep sleeve dec every 3 (3) rnds 0 (1) times more and every 2 (2) rnds 15 (15) times.

Sizes M, L, XL

Rep dec rnd every 3 (3, 3) rnds 1 (2 4) times more and then every 2 (2, 2) rnds 14 (13, 13) times.

All Sizes

Work in k2, p2 rib cont raglan dec every 2 rnds, 4 times—64 (82, 88, 96, 98) sts rem.

Collar

Change to 6.5 mm needle.

Work in k2, p2 rib until piece measures 3 (3, 3, 3½, 3½)"/7.6 (7.6, 7.6, 8.9) cm from beg. BO all sts in patt.

FINISHING

Graft the sleeve and body together at underarms. Block to size. Weave in all ends.

FUTURE ARAN SCHEMATIC

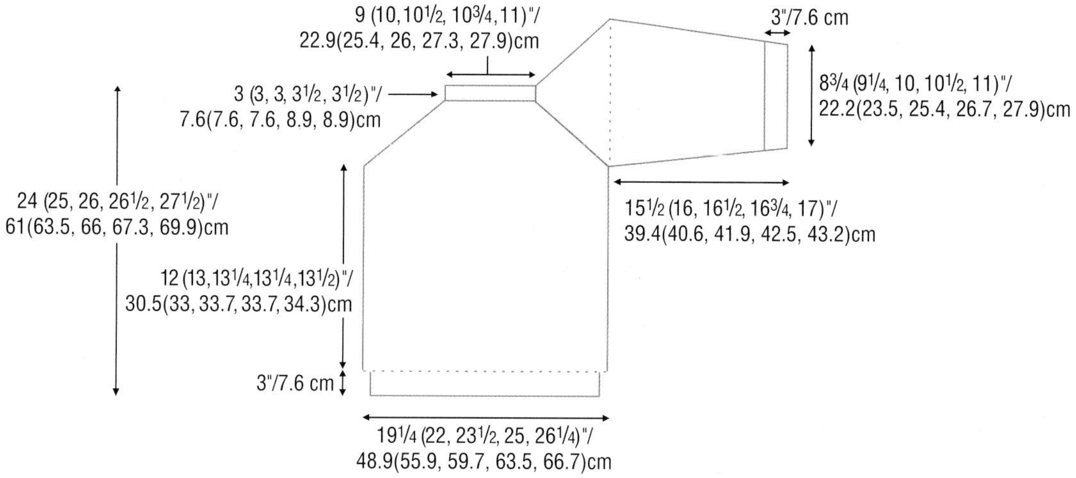
9 (10, 10 1/2, 10 3/4, 11)"/
22.9(25.4, 26, 27.3, 27.9)cm
3"/7.6 cm
3 (3, 3, 3 1/2, 3 1/2)"/
7.6(7.6, 7.6, 8.9, 8.9)cm
8 3/4 (9 1/4, 10, 10 1/2, 11)"/
22.2(23.5, 25.4, 26.7, 27.9)cm
24 (25, 26, 26 1/2, 27 1/2)"/
61(63.5, 66, 67.3, 69.9)cm
15 1/2 (16, 16 1/2, 16 3/4, 17)"/
39.4(40.6, 41.9, 42.5, 43.2)cm
12 (13, 13 1/4, 13 1/4, 13 1/2)"/
30.5(33, 33.7, 33.7, 34.3)cm
3"/7.6 cm
19 1/4 (22, 23 1/2, 25, 26 1/4)"/
48.9(55.9, 59.7, 63.5, 66.7)cm

Appendix

Techniques and Abbreviations

ABBREVIATIONS

b	back
beg	begin(ning)
BO	bind off
cc	contrast color
cn	cable needle
CO	cast on
cont	continue(ing)
dec	decrease(ing)
dpn	double pointed needle(s)
eor	every other row
est	established
f	front
inc	increase(ing)
k	knit
k2tog	knit two together
kfb	knit into front and back
ktbl	knit through back loop
kwise	knitwise
lh	left-hand needle
m(s)	marker (s)
m1	make 1, increase
m1l	With lh needle, lift strand between two needles from front to back. Knit it through front loop.
m1r	With lh needle, lift strand between two needles from back to front. Knit it through back loop.
mc	main color
p	purl
pfb	purl into front and back
pbf	purl into back and front
p2tog	purl 2 together
p2tog tbl	insert right needle up into back loops of the two stitches and purl them together from this position
p/u	pick up
patt	pattern
pm	place marker
psso	pass slip stitch over
p2sso	pass 2 slip stitches over
pwise	purlwise
rh	right-hand needles
RS	right side
rem	remaining
rep	repeat
rev	reverse
rnd(s)	round(s)
sl	slip
sm	slip marker
ssk	slip 2 stitches as if to knit, knit 2 stitches together on left-hand needle
ssp	slip 1 knitwise, slip another knitwise, return slipped stitches to left needle
st(s)	stitch(es)
St st	stockinette stitch
tbl	through back loop
wyib	with yarn in back
wyif	with yarn in front
WS	wrong side
w/t	wrap and turn
yo	yarn over
*	rep directions from *
**	rep directions between ** as directed

KNITTING NEEDLE CONVERSION

Metric (mm)	US	UK/Canada
2.0	0	14
2.25	1	13
2.75	2	12
3.0	-	11
3.25	3	10
3.5	4	-
3.75	5	9
4.0	6	8
4.5	7	7
5.0	8	6
5.5	9	5
6.0	10	4
6.5	10½	3
7.0	10¾	2
7.5	-	1
8.0	11	0
9.0	13	00
10.0	15	000

YARN WEIGHT CHART

YARN WEIGHT SYMBOL & CATEGORY NAMES	0 lace	1 super fine	2 fine	3 light	4 medium	5 bulky	6 super bulky
TYPE OF YARNS IN CATEGORY	Fingering 10-count crochet thread	Sock, Fingering, Baby	Sport, Baby	DK, Light Worsted	Worsted, Afghan, Aran	Chunky, Craft, Rug	Bulky, Roving

Source: Craft Yarn Council of America's www.YarnStandards.com

Special Techniques

Following are some overviews of the techniques used in this book. This isn't a comprehensive guide, but rather a quick and convenient reference, along with details of my favorite way of executing some of these techniques.

BACKWARD LOOP CAST ON

*Loop working yarn and place it on the needle backwards so that it doesn't unwind. Rep from * for specified number of stitches.

CABLING WITHOUT A CABLE NEEDLE

Right Twist

Work to just before the cable stitches begin, move the yarn to the front, and slip half the sts to be cabled purlwise onto the rh needle. Move the yarn across the slipped sts to the back, and knit the second half of the sts to be cabled.

With the lh needle behind the work, insert its tip into the slipped sts. Holding the base of the cable stitches with your left thumb and forefinger, draw the rh needle out of the cable stitches. The slipped stitches will remain on the lh needle, and the worked stitches will be dangling in front of the needle.

From the front, pick up the dangling stitches with the rh needle. The worked stitches are on the rh needle, and the previously slipped stitches are on the lh needle. Move the yarn to the back, and knit the slipped stitches from the lh needle.

Left Twist

Work to just before the cable stitches begin. Move the yarn to the back and slip half the sts to be cabled purlwise on the rh needle. Knit the second half of the stitches to be cabled.

With the lh needle in front of the work, insert its tip into the slipped sts. Holding the base of the cable stitches with your left thumb and forefinger, draw the rh needle out of the cable stitches. The slipped ones will remain on the lh needle, and the worked ones will be dangling at the back of the needle.

From the back, pick up the dangling stitches with the rh needle. The worked stitches are on the rh needle, and the previously slipped stitches are on the lh needle. Knit the previously slipped sts.

I-CORD

Using dpns or circular needles, CO or p/u required number of stitches. *Knit a row. Slide row to other end of needle. Do not turn the work. Pull the yarn around the back of stitches. Rep from *.

INVISIBLE OR PROVISIONAL CAST ON

There are several ways to perform an invisible or provisional cast on. My preferred method is the *chained* version because it's quick, painless, and does not require that stitches be picked up. It's perfect to use with tubular cast ons. I'll admit, though, that for hems, I sometimes simply cast on to two same-sized needles and leave one hanging, so when it's time to knit the stitches together, they are already on a needle.

Using a needle the same size as used for work and cotton waste yarn, make a slip knot onto a crochet hook. *Holding the waste yarn underneath the knitting needle in your left hand, bring the crochet hook over your needle and crochet a chain stitch. Move yarn back under the knitting needle. Repeat from * for required cast-on amount.

KITCHENER STITCH

The trick to this invisible grafting method is to repeat in your head "knit purl, purl knit" as you weave the live stitches. Thread a tapestry needle with a length of yarn that is twice as long as the area to be joined. Hold the needles with the stitches parallel, tips pointing in same direction, and wrong sides of work together.

Setup

Insert tapestry needle into the first st on the front needle as if to purl and pull through, leaving the st on the needle.

Insert tapestry needle into the first st on the back needle as if to knit and pull through, leaving the st on the needle.

Repeats

*Insert needle into the first st on the front needle as if to knit; remove st from needle.

Insert needle into the next st on the front needle as if to purl; leave st on the needle. Draw yarn through. Insert needle into the first st on the back needle as if to purl; remove st from needle.

Insert needle into the next st on the back needle as if to knit; leave st on the needle. Draw yarn through. Rep from * until no sts remain on needles.

MAGIC LOOP METHOD (SMALL CIRCUMFERENCE KNITTING)

This is a great way to knit sleeves in the round if you don't like to use dpns or very short circulars. For this technique, you'll need a circular needle, 32"/81 cm or longer.

Using a circular needle, cast on the required number of stitches. Slide the stitches to the cable, pinch the cable between the two center stitches, and pull it out to create a large loop. Half the stitches will be on one needle and the other half are on the second needle. This is called *home position.* With needle tips pointing to the right, slide the back needle out (stitches will be on cable) and start knitting the stitches on the front needle as usual. At the end of the row (half the round has been completed), turn the work around and return the stitches to home position. The stitches you're about to knit are in front (closest to you), and the yarn attached to the skein is on the right side of the needle in back.

Repeat returning to home position and knitting the stitches in front until all rounds have been completed.

MATTRESS STITCH

Also known as *invisible seaming*, use this to join vertical pieces together for a seamless look. It is worked one stitch in from the edge. To begin, lay the two pieces to be joined side by side with the RS up. Thread a tapestry needle with the same yarn used in the work. Insert the needle into the lowest corner stitch on the left piece from back to front. Then, insert the needle from back to front in the lowest corner stitch on the opposite piece. You have tacked down the yarn and are ready to seam.

Stretch your work a little horizontally, and you'll see a bar between the stitches. Insert the needle under the first two bars and pull through to the RS again. Insert the needle through the parallel bars on the opposite piece. Continue working back and forth in this manner, gently pulling the yarn sometimes to bring the seam together, until you reach the end.

PROVISIONAL CAST ON

Using two yarns, the working yarn and waste yarn, make a loop over the needle, as for a long tail cast-on, using both strands held together. Now, work a long tail cast-on, with the working yarn over your index finger and the waste yarn over your thumb. This way, the stitches on your needles will be in the working yarn, and the waste yarn will be at the bottom edge of the work.

Special Techniques

SHORT ROW SHAPING

Short row, also known as wrap and turn, is used to shape or curve sections of knitting such as heels of socks, shoulders, or collars.

Work to the required number of stitches, and wrap and turn (w/t). To wrap on the knit side, with yarn in back, slip stitch from lh needle purlwise to rh needle, bring yarn between the needles to the front, slip the same stitch back to lh needle, and turn work.

Once the number of short rows in your pattern is completed, you must hide the wraps. The standard way is to work to just before the wrapped stitch, insert the rh needle under the wrap knitwise (or purlwise), and knit (or purl) the stitch and the wrap together.

My friend Joelene taught me an even better way that ensures you'll end up with matching sides and no holes. Pick up the wrap from the bottom and slip on rh needle. Knit the wrapped stitch, and pass the slipped stitch over the knit wrapped stitch.

Wrap the next stitch (this stitch will now have two wraps).

On the purl side, pick up the wrap on the knit side bottom up and slip on rh needle. Purl the wrapped stitch, pass the slipped stitch over the purled wrapped stitch, and wrap the next stitch.

Repeat the process, picking up and passing two wraps, until all stitches are reincorporated.

Shoulder Shaping

For a beautiful, less bulky shoulder seam, combine short rows with a three-needle bind off. When the pattern has you binding off in steps, work short rows instead. The trick is to remember that the right front and left back shoulders are worked with knit side short rows, whereas the left front and right back shoulders are worked with purl side short rows. Work one additional row before starting the shoulder shaping, and work a row to pick up the wraps.

Instead of binding off the pattern stitches, leave those stitches unworked, turning the short row at that spot. For example, if the pattern tells you to BO 5 stitches, then work until there are 5 stitches on lh needle, w/t.

SMOCKING

Smocking involves weaving a needle threaded with yarn up a rib stitch, then inserting the needle through a right rib to a left rib to join them together. Use stitch markers to "pin" ribs in the intervals stated in the pattern, which marks off where to smock. This will allow you to see exactly where to make the stitches.

Thread yarn through a tapestry needle and, beginning with the second knit rib at the lower right edge, pull the needle up through the right side of that rib to the fourth stitch up. Then *insert the needle from right to left through the fourth st of the first and second ribs. Pull the needle through and pull to join the ribs. Rep from * once to complete a smocking stitch.

Pull the needle up through the fourth stitch up on the left side of the second knit rib, and work the smocking stitch, joining the second and third ribs by inserting the needle from left to right.

THREE-NEEDLE BO

With stitches on two needles of the same size and right sides facing, hold the two needles parallel to each other in your left hand and insert a third needle into the first stitch of the front and back needle. Knit these two sts together. *Knit the next two sts together in the same manner. Pass the first st on the third needle over the second st to BO. Rep from * until one st remains. Cut yarn and fasten off by pulling through loop.

TUBULAR CO

Using a needle sized for the rib hem and cotton waste yarn, work chained cast-on (see Invisible Cast-On, earlier) for half the required total stitches plus 1. Switch to main yarn and knit one row (RS), purl one row, knit one row. With WS row facing, *purl first stitch, insert rh needle from top to bottom of first purl stitch in between waste yarn. Place on rh needle going from front to back, and knit this stitch. Repeat from *, ending with a purl stitch. Work k1, p1 ribbing.

TUBULAR OR SEWN BO

A tubular bind off is almost the same as the Kitchener stitch, only in this method the stitches will be on one needle. Thread a tapestry needle (TN) with a length of yarn that is three or four times as long as the length of the row.

Setup

If the first stitch is a knit, insert the TN through the stitch as if to purl, and leave it on the knitting needle.
Insert the TN through the second stitch as if to knit, and pull the yarn through both stitches, leaving both stitches on the knitting needle.
If the first stitch is a purl, put the yarn through the stitch as if to knit and through the second stitch as if to purl.

Repeats

From this point on you will work the stitches according to whether the first stitch on the knitting needle is knit or purl.

If the first stitch is a knit, insert the TN into it for the second time as if to knit, and slip it off the knitting needle. Insert the TN through the next knit stitch as if to purl, and pull the yarn through, but leave the stitches on the knitting needle.

If the first stitch is a purl, insert the TN into the first stitch for the second time as if to purl, and slip it off the knitting needle.

Insert the TN between the next two stitches from the back, and put it through the second stitch on the knitting needle (which is a purl) as if to knit. Pull the yarn through, but leave the stitches on the knitting needle. Repeat until all stitches are bound off.

Designers

LEAH BEAR

Leah lives with her husband in Atlanta, Georgia. She is a certified behavior analyst who works with children with disabilities. When she's not knitting, she can be found in the kitchen channeling Julia Child, hitting the road, or writing all about it on her blog, Between Stupid and Clever (www.betweenstupidandclever.com).

ALLISON BLEVINS

Allison lives in Colorado with her husband and two children. When she is not busy chasing her kids or running her yarn shop, Tangle (store.tangleonline.com), she is knitting! Read about her adventures at her blog, Pretending Sanity (www.pretendingsanity.com).

OLGA BURAYA-KEFELIAN

Olga has been knitting since the age of four and has been creating her own garments for the past nine years. She enjoys the challenge that each garment brings and acquires her inspiration from current runway trends. She lives with her husband and crazy cat in Alexandria, Virginia. You can see more of her everyday knitwear adventures at www.olgajazzzy.com.

CONNIE CHANG CHINCHIO

Connie first started knitting obsessively six years ago in graduate school while studying physics, but has only recently started designing. Her designs have been featured in *Knitter's* magazine and Magknits.com. When her husband can tear her away from her yarn habit, Connie also enjoys hiking, traveling, and cooking. She blogs about her life—knitting and otherwise—at physicsknits.blogspot.com.

KALANI CRAIG

A native of Portland, Oregon, Kalani spent almost 15 years in the Southern California high tech world before returning home to design sweaters and Web sites for the amazing staff at Knit Purl and ShibuiKnits. Kalani is currently a graduate student in medieval history at Indiana University, Bloomington, where she keeps her husband company by reading funny bits of medieval Latin out loud.

WAKANA GATES

Wakana began to knit when she was little, as her mother was a professional knitwear designer and knitting instructor who taught in a studio at her home. Now she is an instructor, too, and has been hosting knitting workshops in New York City. She also works to develop knitting patterns and designs knitwear for a boutique in New York City.

VÉRONIQUE HAEGELI

Véronique became crafty as a young girl—even though her mom couldn't so much as sew a button. As many knitters have, she learned to knit from her grandmother. Alas, at the age of seven, she found knitting tedious and boring. She did, however, leave her native France for New York just in time for the knitting boom and picked up her sticks again. She is now pursuing a career as a neuroscientist by day and a knitting designer by night. Véronique lives in Brooklyn surrounded by bins upon bins of yarn and fellow knitting enthusiasts. You can follow her knitting adventures at treschicveronique.blogspot.com.

Designers

SARAH HEINIGER

Sarah comes from a family of crafty women. They were quilting, crocheting, and cross-stitching since before she was born. But none of them knit! After trying all of those crafts and then some, she picked up the needles on her own one day and has never looked back. All that knitting led to a desire to stretch her muscles and design a bit. She has always loved classic silhouettes and cables, and so it just seemed natural that such a piece would be her first published work. She lives and works just outside of Chicago and archives her knitting progress on her blog, Persnickety (persnickety.blogspirit.com).

STEPHANIE PULFORD

Stef was but a wee child when she took up the needles. Twenty years later, she masquerades as a mild-mannered grad student by day. By night she dons a (knitted) cape and defends Davis, California, from the forces of evil. She also blogs at www.knitthehellup.com.

ERIKA SEELINGER

An obsession with Dale of Norway's fabulous Lillehammer Olympic Team sweater and Alafoss Lopi inspired Scandiaphile Erika to learn to knit in 2004. Since becoming a continental-style knitter, she has gained a passion for texture and a mountain of sock yarn. She recently returned from a trip to the Bavarian and Tyrolean Alps that inspired the Pilatus set. Trained in industrial design, these days Erika can be found sweating it out in central Arizona, working in the IT industry, wandering the aisles at IKEA, and dreaming of her next trip to Scandinavia.

LUCINDA SNYDER

Lucinda Snyder is founder and owner of Wild Wools in Rochester, New York. An avid knitter, Lucinda began designing pieces of her own to wear in her shop. As her designs began to debut, customer interest for her patterns grew. Seeing an opportunity to join the growing forces of emerging designers willing to push the boundaries of traditional knitting, Lucinda began gathering sketches and ideas. By late 2006, a few sketches morphed into a collection of 17 patterns, and Modalura presented the first release of her pattern designs.

KATE SONNICK

Kate's grandmother taught her to knit when she was six. Her first project: knitting bandages for the leopards. (It wasn't till much later that she learned the bandages were actually for *lepers*, not leopards.) Her knitting continues its wild turn even today. The creator of the Wild Woolies viral knitting campaign (gowildforknitting.blogspot.com), Kate is also a freelance advertising writer and creative director. You can follow Kate's knitting, designs, and ideas at knitlit.blogspot.com.

ANDREA TUNG

Andrea Tung is the founder of Fable Handknit (fablehandknit.com), a luxury yarn company. She has a degree in fashion design from Ryerson University and writes a fashion and knitting blog, Making Things (andreatung.blogspot.com).

ZOË VALETTE

Zoë has recently relocated to Michigan after spending several years in New Jersey. She teaches ballroom dancing and also manages to find time to knit, sew, crochet, and design. She is the kind of knitter who knits at the checkout line! When not knitting, she can be found outside in her garden or chasing after her dog and cats. In the winter, she can be found curled up on the couch with a good book and some knitting. She loves to travel, and her favorite place to knit is in the car on a road trip.

ILLANNA WEINER

Illanna loves to knit in her new home in Brooklyn, New York. She finds design inspiration in nature, architecture, movies, songs, stories, and, of course, yarn. Her favorite fiber comes from sheep, and her favorite needles come from Germany. When Illanna puts down her knitting, she enjoys sketching sweater ideas and singing along to the radio.

MELISSA WEHRLE

Melissa learned how to knit when she was seven years old, but it didn't really stick until she majored in Fashion Design at the Fashion Institute of Technology. A 2002 FIT graduate, she currently works as a knitwear designer for a sweater manufacturer in New York City. In her free time, she designs handknit patterns for a number of small yarn companies, magazines, and for her own line of patterns. To follow her current projects and designs in progress, visit her knitting blog at neoknits.blogspot.com.

About the Author

Yahaira Ferreira is the author of *Sensual Knits*. She learned to knit from her mother-in-law while receiving her M.F.A in photography at the Savannah College of Art & Design. Her background in photography gives her a sophisticated eye for colors, textures, and shapes. A passionate knitter, Yahaira saw a need for luxurious and hard-to-find yarns, and so she launched her boutique website, PureKnits (www.pureknits.com). Yahaira lives in Blackwood, New Jersey with her husband and Boston Terrier. To follow her knitting adventures, visit her blog at www.bitterpurl.com.

Acknowledgments

Even though my name is the only one on the cover of this book, it took the help of a small group of people to get me there. Tom, as always, gave me the support I needed to work on my writing and knitting—thanks for the space and time. Heaps of gratitude to all the designers, who not only managed to design beautiful projects, but completed them under tight deadlines (especially Stephanie Anesi, who, somehow, was able to speed through a lace sweater on small needles in record time for the photo shoot!). The projects in this book wouldn't be possible if it weren't for the generous yarn companies who shipped yarns all over the country. Finally, thanks to the team at Lark Books for all their hard work towards putting this book on the shelves.

Index